EAM

Yours sincerely
Agnes B Marshall

VICTORIAN ICES & ICE CREAM

117 delicious and unusual recipes updated for the modern kitchen

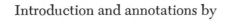

Original recipes from

THE BOOK OF ICES
by
A. B. MARSHALL
London, 1885

Introduction and annotations by

BARBARA KETCHAM WHEATON

Foreword by

A. HYATT MAYOR

THE METROPOLITAN MUSEUM OF ART

CHARLES SCRIBNER'S SONS

New York

I would like to thank the staffs of the Schlesinger Library of Radcliffe College, the Microtext Division of the Harvard College Library, and the Boston Public Library for their assistance. Gillian and David Steel carried out inquiries in London for which I am very grateful. I would like to thank Robie Rogge, of The Metropolitan Museum of Art, whose enthusiasm and assistance have made my researches a pleasure.

FRONT COVER:
"Luncheon table laid under tent, for fetes, &c." (detail)

BACK COVER:
"Artistically served ices" (detail)

Chromolithographs from *Encyclopaedia of Practical Cookery,* edited by Theodore Francis Garrett. Published by L. Upcot Gill, London, 1898. General Research Division, The New York Public Library, Astor, Lenox and Tilden Foundations

Printed in the United States of America
Designed by Peter Oldenburg

Victorian Ices & Ice Cream was first published in 1976 by The Metropolitan Museum of Art under the title *Ices, Plain and Fancy.*

LIBRARY OF CONGRESS CATALOGING IN PUBLICATION DATA

Marshall, A. B. (Agnes B.)
    Victorian ices & ice cream.

    1. Ice cream, ices, etc.   I. Wheaton, Barbara Ketcham.   II. Title.   III. Title: Victorian ices and ice cream.
TX795.M293   1984   641.8'62   84-14739
ISBN 0-87099-409-3
ISBN 0-684-18267-x (Scribner)

Foreword

A public print collection in a metropolis operates like a public library, which offers, besides Homer, Dante, and Shakespeare, also the books that help doctors, plumbers, lawyers, historians, and all the innumerable specialists who make up the greatness of a city. A print collection is a library of images whose foundation is the work of supreme artists like Rembrandt and Dürer, but which must also answer the infinite special needs of its public. One of the most fascinating of the many specialities in the Metropolitan Museum's print collection is the section of what print jargon calls "ornament"—the prints that record decorative designs or supply them to silversmiths, cabinetmakers, jewelers, architects, and even pastry cooks. Within this specialty the Museum has collected a sub-specialty to document the American Wing with illustrated trade catalogues of the domestic and foreign things that the Wing has collected or may one day start to collect. Much of this section consists of the mail-order catalogues that England invented around 1760. There are even more of the American catalogues that sold goods since the early days of the United States, throughout a vast territory where a not quite impossible postal system moved merchandise without the hurdles of customs barriers or differences of currency. The Museum has carefully selected these catalogues to record the history of living conditions and the development of taste. They are also the graphic documents for the all-important history of commerce. When Mrs. Marshall dished up an exotic American wine sorbet in crystal ice cups, it was to promote the sale of her special tin molds, but we bless her book today for taking us back to an age when Victorian and Edwardian Englishmen and Americans could bury their troubles in a dish of ice cream snuggling under a dollop of whipped cream in blissful ignorance of calories and cholesterol.

This stately eating and its portly consequences left a living memorial in two sets of photographs that illustrate this book. One set is selected from Associate Curator Weston Naef's collection of stereoscopic views of American soda fountains and spas, adorned like altars dedicated to indulgence and contrition. The other set comes out of the family album of the witty and resourceful designer of the Museum's books, Peter Oldenburg. These images bring us THE FAMILY as a corporation almost priestly in the simple seriousness of its eating. Some of these family rituals took place in Germany, but they would have been the same anywhere in the Western world during any of the decades just before the First World War. Looking back at those faces so sure of tomorrow gives us the comfort that confidence has to return some day to cheer us once again.

A. HYATT MAYOR
Curator Emeritus
Department of Prints and Photographs

Introduction

"The cook was a good cook, as cooks go; and as cooks go, she went," wrote Saki (H. H. Munro). The writer's neighbor on Mortimer Street in London, Agnes B. Marshall, may have given her that mobility. With her husband, Alfred William Marshall, this versatile woman operated a cooking school and an employment agency for superior cooks; she had a store which sold kitchen equipment, some of it of her own design; she sold imported and specialty foods, lectured, and published a weekly paper and four cookbooks. *The Book of Ices* was her first. It appeared in 1885, the same year that she introduced her patent ice-cream freezer and "ice cave," or storage box.

In 1883, she took over the Mortimer Street School of Cookery, which had been run since 1857 by Felix and Mary Anne Lavenue. By 1885 she was giving lecture demonstrations five or six days a week. Already her shop was offering a wide range of kitchen equipment. She had her name embossed on most of the cast-iron items she sold; similarly, it was pressed into the glass of her bottles of flavorings and colors. The reader of *The Book of Ices* will observe that the contents of these bottles are used lavishly. Agnes Marshall never forgot any of her enterprises for a moment. We may be sure that the gas stove she cooked on was of the same make that was sold in her store. The walls of her classroom bore advertisements for her penny paper, *The Table,* for her leaf gelatin, for *The Book of Ices.* The wooden drums of baking powder she sold contained coupons which could be collected and exchanged for copies of her books. Her later books require the use of recipes available only in the earlier ones, a feature which she puts in a favorable light by pointing out that she thus avoids repetition. All of her cookbooks call for extensive use of her food products and kitchen equipment, and all of them conclude with a section of advertisements showing extracts from her sales catalogues. She offered more than a thousand varieties and sizes of molds alone; *The Book of Ices* and, later, her *Fancy Ices* must have helped to sell them. The advertisements include descriptions of her school and extensive quotations from favorable press notices, of which there were many.

It is not surprising, then, that the appearance of *The Book of Ices* coincided with the introduction of her patent freezer, and that on page two she recommends that the reader attend a lesson on ices at her school. Most ice-cream freezers, then and now, are deep and narrow. Mrs. Marshall's patent machine was broad and shallow, a proportion which has recently come into use again, for in-the-food-freezer electric models. Before the first public lesson at which she demonstrated her machine, she made the extravagant claim, in an advertisement in the *Times* of London, that in three minutes it would make ice cream, which her patent "ice cave" would keep cold "from one day to another." After the first public lesson she reduced the storage period to twelve hours, although in her book she says that ice cream can be kept in the "ice cave" overnight.

Ice-cream desserts enjoyed considerable social esteem at the time, because they called for expensive ingredients, special equipment, careful timing, and the attentions of a skilled cook. Often ices were bought, as they are today, rather than made at home. Throughout the nineteenth century and into the twentieth, Gunter's was the pre-eminent supplier of ices for upper-class dinners in London. Similarly, among the proliferating cookery schools of the day, Mrs. Marshall's was distinguished by being predominantly for cooks serving upper-class tables. The National Training School for Cookery, an ancestor of home-economics schools, trained teachers of cooking. Individuals with special skills offered more specialized instruction: an English colonel returned from India gave lessons in curries; "a French cordon-bleu" had classes for ladies who wished to do French cooking. Mrs. Marshall addressed

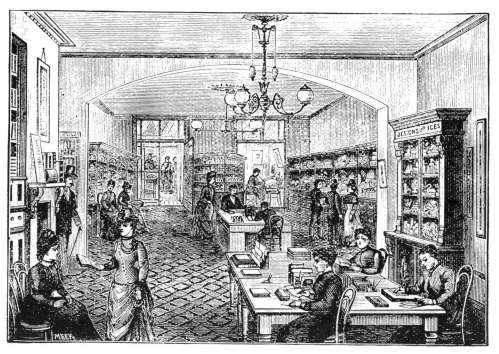

Mrs. A. B. Marshall's School of Cookery. Show Room for Moulds, Cooks' Knives, Cutlery, &c.

herself especially to domestics serving in upper-class households; her lectures were attended by female cooks "and their ladies." Her notices in the *Times* describe the kind of cookery she taught as "high-class cookery, French and English." This may explain why she is so little known today. French cooking is in style, and so is regional peasant cooking, but her recipes are neither. Mrs. Marshall's style of cookery is very true to what was being eaten by prosperous Londoners in her day. The last thing on earth a hostess would offer her guest was a Lancashire hot pot, however succulent; some of W. S. Gilbert's "not too French" French beans would have been much more appropriate.

In the United States, too, ices were considered a superior dessert for the best dinner tables, whether in private homes or in restaurants. In New York City, Delmonico's and, later, Sherry's, which were probably America's most famous restaurants, made a specialty of them. Charles Ranhofer, the chef at Delmonico's from 1862 until 1894, made all sorts of ice creams and elaborate desserts constructed with ice cream. He has been credited with the invention of baked Alaska. In his immense cookbook, *The Epicurean* (1894), he calls it an Alaska or a Florida, and makes it in individual portions. A tall cone, half of banana ice cream and half of vanilla, is set into a disk of firm cake, which has been slightly hollowed out and lined with apricot marmalade; it is kept frozen until the last possible minute, then covered with flutings of meringue, browned rapidly in a hot oven, and served immediately. Ranhofer is said to have invented it to commemorate Seward's purchase of Alaska in 1867. Mrs. Mary F. Henderson, in her *Practical Cooking and Dinner Giving* (1876), calls it "German Steamer Baked Ice-cream." She shows some familiarity with Delmonico's, and gives a recipe for their vanilla ice cream. Is it possible that what Ranhofer deserves is the credit for popularizing an already known dessert? So far as I know, the credit for inventing truffle ice cream is entirely his; it is used as a garnish for a rice ice cream not unlike Mrs. Marshall's. It is a very odd recipe: the custard is prepared with cream infused with truffles; from it a rich ice cream is made, frozen in chocolate-lined, truffle-shaped molds, and rolled in chopped truffles. It is a triumph of skill and imagination over taste and good sense. Another of his oddities, asparagus ice cream, is similar to Mrs. Marshall's spinach and cucumber ices. He offers two versions, one made with asparagus ice cream, the other with pistachio and vanilla ice cream; in either case the ice-cream spears are tied together with pink ribbon.

While the modern diner may well be puzzled at the state of mind which produces vegetable ice creams, a brief consideration of the late-nineteenth-century menu shows how this came about. The formal Victorian dinner was long, lasting two or even three hours, and consisted of many courses. Ices could appear in two or even three of them. The meal was divided into two parts. A soup course came first; usually the diner had the choice of a thick soup or a clear consommé. Three courses followed: fish, entrée, and relévé or remove. The latter was a large roast garnished with vegetables. The second part of the meal opened with a sorbet or a punch—a water ice

Show Rooms: 32 Mortimer Street, W., for Kitchen Furnishings, and French, Italian, and American Goods.

flavored with rum or other spirits—thus contrasting with the hot liquid at the beginning of the meal. Then the diner went on to successive courses of more roast meat, vegetables, and sweets. In her *Cookery Book* Mrs. Marshall describes the character of a sorbet:

> Under the term sorbet are now included those ices which are served after the removes. They should be of a light semi-frozen nature, having only just sufficient consistency to hold together when piled up. This degree of solidity is a natural consequence of their composition, for the sugar and spirit among their ingredients, when properly prepared, will prevent them, under any circumstances, becoming as solid as cream and water ices. They are generally prepared by first making an ordinary lemon-water ice, and adding to this some spirit, liqueur, or syrup for flavouring, and fruit for garnish, and are named accordingly rum sorbet, cherry sorbet, and so on. They are always served in cups or glasses, one for each guest, and many very pretty designs are specially made for this purpose.

The coldness and granular texture of the sorbet, the acidity of the lemon juice, and the slight bitterness from the infused lemon peel provide a refreshing contrast to the heat and the unctuous textures of preceding courses. Just how elaborate the "pretty designs" could be is illustrated by Ranhofer's "Stanley Punch," a very liquid sorbet made with coffee, lemons, kirsch, maraschino, and meringue. The punch was served "inside of a goblet beside which is a heron made of gum paste surrounded by grasses." Presumably the diner could imagine himself an African explorer foraging for his dinner.

As the Victorian meal drew to a close, the *entremet* course was served. Nowadays this is understood to mean the dessert, but in Mrs. Marshall's day it included vegetables as well, and even the savoury seems originally to have belonged in it. Each diner chose whatever appealed to him from the selection offered; it was not expected that anyone would want to take helpings of everything. The *entremets* demonstrated by Mrs. Marshall at an "Entire Dinner Lesson" at her school in 1892 included a dish of cardoons (a vegetable with celery-like stalks, related to the artichoke) with beef

View of Mrs. A. B. Marshall's Class Room during the progress of an Entire Dinner Lesson on May 6, 1887.

[xiii]

marrow; small baskets of nougat "à la Dürer"; *bombe à la portugaise* (a molded dessert of rum and peach ice, lined with kirsch cream ice, garnished with maidenhair fern and spun sugar); and a savoury (*petites croustades à la Victoria*). In such mixed company a cucumber ice would hardly be out of place.

Mrs. Marshall's enthusiasm warms when she describes the sweets:

> The aim of a properly constructed sweet is to convey to the palate the greatest possible amount of pleasure and taste, whilst it is in no way either suggestive of nourishment or solidity. . . . Of late ices and iced dishes of various kinds have increased so much in popular favour as to form a special, and decidedly important item, at every well arranged dinner. . . . At large parties two sorts of ices are usually served, and should be carefully contrasted. A pleasing variety is often produced by filling little moulds with different kinds of ice, which are then served in tiny lace paper cups, under the name of *glaces assorties,* or else the different colours and flavours are placed in the same mould either regularly or not; in the latter case they produce a marbled effect, suggestive of the Venetian glass known as millefiori or 'colorito.' Another very popular form is the Neapolitan ice, or crème panachée as it is sometimes called, which is produced by filling a metal box, made for the purpose, with layers of differently flavoured and coloured cream and water ices; for instance, lemon, vanilla, chocolate, and pistachio. When moulded these are turned out, cut across in slices, and, served in little paper lace cases, offer the requisite variety to both sight and palate.

The Book of Ices was followed, in 1888, by *Mrs. A. B. Marshall's Cookery Book,* a long, general-purpose cookbook, of which eventually sixty thousand copies were sold. She interspersed authorship with repeated remodelings of her shop and classrooms, and, in the 1880s, with an ambitious series of lecture tours. Her demonstration lecture "A Pretty Luncheon" was seen in many of England's principal towns, often under the patronage of titled ladies. These tours brought her favorable notice in the newspapers, an advantage she was quick to exploit. The pinnacle of recognition came when a special London lecture was noticed in the *Times*:

> A crowded audience, which filled to its utmost capacity the large banqueting hall of Willis's Rooms [a respectable restaurant near St. James's Palace] assembled on Satur-

day afternoon to hear Mrs. A. B. Marshall demonstratively explain several of the operations of high-class cookery, and to watch her prepare many *recherché* dishes, which she classified together under the title "A Pretty Luncheon." In a few clear words Mrs. Marshall explained what she intended to do, and how she proposed to proceed, and for two hours she completely engrossed the earnest attention of some 600 people, instructing and entertaining them at the same time. At the end of the lecture, or performance, whichever it may be called, her labours elicited a unanimous outburst of applause.

On another occasion a reporter observed:

Mrs. Marshall wastes nothing. She does not even waste words; still less does she waste time. When her luncheon is finished her work is done. There is no litter behind to clear up.

Anyone who cooks can appreciate the advantages of so methodical a way of working; not everyone can achieve it.

A trip to the United States in the summer of 1888 was less successful. She returned without any usable newspaper articles, although she was briefly noticed by the *Philadelphia Evening Bulletin* as "the Miss Parloa of England." Maria Parloa, who had studied at the National Training School of Cookery in London, was one of the original teachers at the Boston Cooking School. The newspaper described Mrs. Marshall as "a brunette of fine form and bearing, under middle age, with the ruddy complexion that characterizes English women. She is a fluent talker and speaks with a marked English accent." She did return with some new recipes to put in her next cookbook, *Mrs. A. B. Marshall's Larger Cookery Book of Extra Recipes* (1891). In it we find Philadelphia doughnuts and Chicago doughnuts, flannel cakes, Saratoga potato chips, and a recipe for corn on the cob. If she did not succeed in popularizing the last, we need not be surprised. She boiled the corn for an hour, then served it cold, masked with a mayonnaise-like sauce to which were added puréed oysters. This new book was dedicated to Helena, Princess Christian of Schleswig-Holstein, a daughter of Queen Victoria. Mrs. Marshall had given dinners, "with vaudeville entertainment," for the poor in the East End of London; Princess Christian also concerned herself with feeding the hungry. Thus it came about that, in the spring of 1888, Mrs. Marshall gave "a fully-illustrated practical lecture on high-class cookery" in London, under the patronage of the Princess, "in aid of the Board School Children's Free Dinner Fund."

Her career as an entrepreneur and teacher continued until her death in 1905 at the age of fifty. Her husband and the school survived her, the latter continuing on Mortimer Street until the early 1950s.

What is most notable about Agnes Marshall is the way in which she was able to span so many divisions of English society. We may smile at her relentless promotion of her enterprises, but the work she did served the needs of people in many classes. Wealthy hostesses in need of temporary or permanent cooks, middle-class women who wanted to set fashionable tables, ambitious young women in domestic service— Mrs. Marshall served them all.

What could a student at Mrs. Marshall's school hope to get in return for a course of study which might cost £22 for twelve weeks, at a time when an ordinary cook earned that much in a year? Cooks and other domestic servants were remunerated according to skill. Advertisements in the *Times* of London placed by cooks looking for work, and by employers and employment agencies (including Mrs. Marshall's) looking for cooks, used a standardized terminology to describe those levels of skill. A "plain cook" could earn £15 to £20 a year (in addition to room and board) and would be expected to do all the kitchen work herself, as well as keep the dining room clean, set the table, and do the washing up. If her post was in the country, she would also be responsible for the dairy. As soon as she was experienced enough to describe herself as a "good plain cook," she specified "no dairy work." Employers, in turn, could set stringent requirements with respect to religious belief and drinking habits, and even the height of parlormaids and footmen; and, at one moment in the history of hairdressing, an advertisement stipulated "no fringe." But if a cook could, by hard work, skill, and good luck, raise herself to the level of a "thorough good cook" or a "first rate cook-housekeeper," she would be able to insist on having the help of one or more kitchenmaids, and could aspire to annual wages of £50 to £60, as well as the more ample perquisites of a wealthy house. Olga Manders, the cook for Rumer Godden, the novelist, studied at Marshall's School. She recalls what attracted her to her career; early in her work as a housemaid she had observed of the cook in a large establishment that, after the butler, "she [was] the most important person on the domestic side of the family, queen in her own territory, with no need to kowtow to anyone. . . ." The geographic mobility of cooks remarked on by Saki was an outward reflection of the much more important social mobility which having a skill gave to working people.

Although Mrs. Marshall is a lucid writer, she is not overscrupulous in her borrowings from other writers. In her *Cookery Book*, in the chapter discussing menu composition, there are passages taken verbatim from *Kettner's Book of the Table* (1877), but she can and does claim that "every recipe has been carried out by Mrs. A. B. Marshall and written out by her accordingly. None are copied from other books." She does not think it necessary to mention that she has cribbed some of her table of contents for *The Book of Ices* from William Jeanes's *Gunter's Modern Confectioner* (1867). It is not surprising that she would want to give recipes for Gunter's ices. Since the days of George III, this confectionery shop had enjoyed the highest patronage, and Gunter's ices were the standard by which all others would be judged. Copying from Jeanes's list, however, led Mrs. Marshall into two errors. Of blackcurrant ice water, she says that "this is made in the same manner as the barberry ice water," but she gives no recipe for the latter. Jeanes does, using a pint of berries boiled in half a pint of water, then sieved, mixed with an equal quantity of syrup, and frozen. She also borrows an outright mistake from him: neither his "grape" water ice nor hers contains any grapes. It is made with clusters of elderflowers, which in French are *grappes de sureau*. Mrs. Marshall's recipes, however, are very different from Jeanes's. His are often twice as sweet, and his instructions are less clearly worded. Moreover, between the appearance of *Gunter's Modern Confectioner* and the publication of *The Book of Ices,* an important innovation in the making of ice cream had taken place: the crank-type freezer arrived from the United States. It is said to have been invented by an American woman, one Nancy Johnson, in 1846. Paul Dickson, in *The Great American Ice Cream Book* (1972), writes that "for reasons that have never been made clear, Nancy Johnson did not patent her invention, and on May 30, 1848, William G. Young registered it with the Patent Office. Young at least had the courtesy to call his product the 'Johnson Patent Ice-Cream Freezer.'" It quickly replaced the old hand-stirred process; Mrs. Marshall gives a description of the effort involved:

> Formerly the manufacture of ices was a tedious and difficult operation, requiring an expensive apparatus and considerable skill and goodwill on the part of the operator to ensure success: each mould being embedded in a mixture of salt, ice, and saltpetre, had to be luted down [sealed] with wax, or fat of some kind, and unless this was very carefully applied and as carefully removed, the ice was apt, on being taken from the mould, to acquire an unpleasant salt taste, such as many may remember. Moreover, to stand the treatment necessary the moulds required to be of a particular make, and were in consequence costly, while the whole process was so troublesome as to be scarcely worth the result in establishments where ices were not of constant occurrence. But with the improved apparatus of the present day they have become comparatively inexpensive and easily made luxuries, in even small establishments.

She goes on to describe the superior qualities of her own brand of freezers and storage boxes; she might have added that often, with the old method, the mixture was scraped down from the sides of the mold with a "spaddle," a long wooden instrument with a little shovel at the end, and then worked until smooth. The mixture was then refrozen. Deep, smooth-sided freezing pots were used, so that the spaddle could scrape the congealed ice cream away from the sides of the pot, working it into a creamy mixture as the freezing pot was swirled around in the ice and salt. The ice cream was often packed for mellowing into another, deeply fluted mold, whose large proportion of surface area relative to its volume allowed rapid firming.

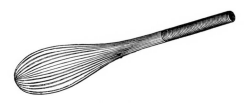

Mrs. Marshall's recipes are practical, and most of them are delicious. No experience is needed, and no great investment in equipment. Making ice cream is not at all like performing magic rituals; there is a great deal of room for experiment and adaptation. *The Book of Ices* may be used in two different ways by the twentieth-century cook. To taste Victorian flavors, one will follow the recipes exactly. Or, to give variety to a repertory of modern ice creams, the cook may vary them with some of Agnes Marshall's ideas. All kinds of fruit and fruit jams and syrups make good water ices, and many are delicious in the custard and cream ices. Liqueurs, even the more bizarre ones, if discreetly used, can have something to contribute. Different flavors of ice cream combine well with each other. Bombes repay the cook's effort generously, and every household should have its own *bombe maison*. Mrs. Marshall's are worth considering:

> White coffee and strawberry cream
> Vanilla cream and strawberry, raspberry, or cherry water
> Brown-bread and chocolate creams
> Tea cream (*crème de thé*) and burnt-almond cream
> Almond and black-currant cream (*crème de cassis*)

The textures produced by the recipes in *The Book of Ices* are much more varied than the textures of modern frozen desserts. There are sumptuously smooth custards, slightly grainy frozen creams, and sorbets with the consistency of slushy snow; one learns that things can melt in the mouth in a great variety of ways. The differences in richness are striking, too. The rich, custard-based ice creams exactly fit our modern idea of Victorian food, but we have been led by our preconceptions to overlook the great variety of textures, of tartness, flavors, and combinations which were then and still are possible. The water ices are acid; their flavors are intense. They are as welcome at the end of a rich meal as they are unexpected.

One of the many advantages of homemade ice cream is that its degree of richness may be adjusted to the needs of a particular flavor and of a particular meal by selecting the fatness of the cream, or cream and milk mixture, and varying the quantity of egg yolks. The nut ice creams, for example, are made with large amounts of egg yolk; therefore the cook will probably choose to use light cream, or cream and milk, because anything richer would be excessively fat. On the other hand, the richness of a custard made entirely with cream combines very well with coffee or liqueurs. The substantial flavor of chocolate can fill out the lightness of a mixture that contains little or no cream. You may choose to make the fruit ice creams either light or rich according to what has already been served. Peach combines well with light cream, but at the end of a light meal you might choose a custard base instead. Whenever fruit is used it should be entirely ripe, with its flavor fully developed.

The basic cream-ice recipes Agnes Marshall gives us, Numbers 1 through 5, allow the cook a great deal of control over expense, richness, and flavor. It should be noted, though, that even the most expensive ingredients will cost little more than an equivalent amount of high-quality commercial ice cream. Indeed, the simpler cream ices and the water ices will usually cost less to make than they would to buy—if they were obtainable. Mrs. Marshall's first base custard, "Very Rich," is indeed sumptuous and should be used for festive occasions. Number 2, "Ordinary," is an ideal all-purpose ice-cream base, nearly as rich as the first when it is made with a large proportion of cream, or lighter if only milk is used. The generous quantity of egg yolks in it guarantees a deliciously smooth ice cream. It is especially good with nuts. When made with milk rather than cream, though still good, it does not accord with the Department of Agriculture's definition of ice cream. Neither does "Common," but the gelatin in it produces a surprisingly agreeable light ice, which is very good in a sugar cone. Number 4, "Cheap," makes a tasty frozen dessert rather like a milk sherbet; crushed fruit is good with it. Number 5, "Plain Cream Ice," is like Philadelphia ice cream. It does not, however, contain the dash of salt which gives the latter its unusual quality.

These recipes can be a revelation to the modern palate, jaded as it is with monotonous, artificially flavored and preserved commercial ice creams. Even the most resolutely modern cook should try some of these recipes in their pure form. Many of the more exotic-sounding ingredients are not very difficult to locate, and there are reasonable substitutes. The techniques are simpler now, because we have so much useful machinery. No longer is the cook obliged to spend hours rubbing fruit through horsehair sieves or through a tammy cloth, or pounding nuts in a mortar. The equipment you already have in your kitchen will be enough. A hand-operated food mill makes splendid purées; the French kind with three interchangeable grids is especially useful, since it allows a choice of textures. If you have a blender

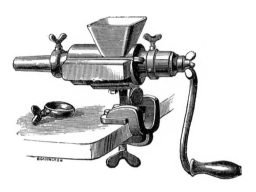

Paragon Mincer

you will probably use it for purées, chopping nuts, and making bread crumbs. The food processor will do all of these things. Occasionally you may still want to run a purée through a sieve to make sure that the blender or processor has left no oversized lumps. Very small pieces of crushed fruit are good in ice cream; large ones freeze into disagreeable lumps. A discreet quantity of chopped or slivered nuts may be stirred into an ice cream after its initial freezing.

As we have seen, some of Mrs. Marshall's best ice creams are made with custards; the cook who avoids making them because they might curdle is being unnecessarily cautious. In making a "boiled" custard (which must *not*, in fact, boil), I always insure against curdling by keeping a bowl of cold water next to the stove. Then, if the mixture begins to thicken too quickly, I can stop the cooking immediately by plunging the bottom of the pan into cold water. A curdled custard, however, will do your ice cream very little harm. I deliberately brought a batch of custard (Number 2) to a full boil, and the ice cream made from it was nearly indistinguishable from ice cream made in the usual way. In fact, my advice to the novice custard cook would be to plan to make ice cream regularly, until curdling becomes unthinkable.

In modern ice-cream recipes, some techniques are different. We make them smoother with meringue; fruit is not added until the freezing process is half done. But Mrs. Marshall's recipes will nearly always work as they are written (I have noted a few changes in the margins), and it is useful to be reminded that in the kitchen there are often several different ways of achieving satisfactory results. Mrs. Marshall uses food coloring to excess, even putting carmine in the cranberry ice, and sometimes she prefers her kirsch and maraschino flavoring syrups to the real kirsch and maraschino which they imitate. The Victorians did like intense and rather heavy colors. Remembering, moreover, that Mrs. Marshall was a persistent saleswoman, we will do as we please.

The modern cook can choose from a variety of freezing equipment. For the soufflés, mousses, and muscovites, which are still-frozen, only a food freezer is needed. I have also made ice cream which is meant to be stir-frozen by putting it in a metal bowl in the food freezer and stirring the mixture vigorously for one minute every half hour. The resulting ice cream is not so smooth as that made in a crank freezer, but it still tastes better than any that can be bought. I would urge anyone who lacks the storage space for an ice-cream freezer to try this simple alternative. In testing Mrs. Marshall's recipes I used two different electric ice-cream makers. One machine is set directly in the food freezer; it has the short, horizontal proportions of Mrs. Marshall's freezer and has a capacity of about one quart. (Many of the recipes in this book make larger quantities, but it is a simple matter to halve them.) The canister is three inches deep; like all stir-freezing containers, it should not be filled to more than two-thirds its capacity. The freezing process is a very simple one: after the machine is filled and assembled, it is set in the food freezer and plugged in. It is supposed to turn itself off when the ice cream is frozen, but I have found that with the light water ice and sorbet mixtures it may not do so. Do not go out for the day and leave it running.

The second machine I used is the old-fashioned sort, consisting of an inner canister for the ice cream, set into a tub containing a mixture of crushed ice and rock salt. Mine has an electrically driven motor; it does not turn itself off but must be unplugged when the ice cream reaches the desired consistency. The process is fairly quick; half an hour's freezing will finish most of the ices. This machine has a capacity of six quarts but can make small quantities as well. It requires crushed ice; ice cubes prevent the canister from turning smoothly and will not provide enough cooling. An electric ice crusher reduces the four or five trays of ice cubes needed to an excellent texture in just a few minutes. A hand-operated crusher will do the same job. Some prodigal souls recommend putting the ice cubes in a pillow case and hammering them, but this is useful only if you want to destroy your pillow cases. A sturdy canvas bag will last longer but may not be so easy to find. The usual proportion for freezing is six or eight parts of crushed ice to one part of rock salt. I measured quantities the first two or three times I made ice cream, but now I simply guess. In emergencies I have successfully substituted kosher salt for rock salt.

Patent Ice Breaker

After the ice cream has been frozen to a fairly firm consistency, it is taken out of the freezing machine and packed into a storage container or a mold to mellow for a few hours. Storage now is much easier than in the past, when the ice cream had to be mellowed in a second batch of crushed ice and salt. Homemade ice creams do not have the keeping qualities of the commercial varieties; this is the price we pay for omitting preservatives and chemical compounds. Homemade ice creams are best frozen the day they are to be eaten, although the basic mixture may be made up the day before and kept, well chilled, until it is time to freeze it. The usual tasting a careful cook does

Swan Mould

must take into account the effect of cold on flavors. Sweetness diminishes as liquids cool, and the balance among flavors alters. An ice-cream mixture that tastes exactly right before it is frozen may be insipid afterwards. Just keep tasting, and you will learn how to adjust flavors to your own liking.

Ice cream lends itself splendidly to decorative presentation. No sensible diner will feel at all cheated by a plain dish of homemade ice cream, "served rough," as Agnes Marshall puts it. On the other hand, people always like to see an ornamental dessert. Fancy molds are excellent for decorative effects. Modern aluminum copies of old lead individual molds can be found; a variety of shapes makes a very pretty sight on the table. Tinned iron molds sometimes discolor red fruits such as rasp-

Rose Mould

berries or strawberries, and no worn tinned copper mold should ever be used, because of the danger of poisoning. Ordinary mixing bowls and loaf pans make perfectly satisfactory substitutes for molds.

The larger a mold is, the longer it will take to set firm. Mrs. Marshall's recommended freezing times should be disregarded; each cook will work out timings suitable to his or her own kitchen. An ice cream made in the morning and molded in the early afternoon will be quite ready to serve in the evening. To make a bombe, an outer layer of very firm ice cream is pressed into place in a chilled mold with the back of a spoon. The mold is put in the freezer until it is quite firm; then the filling can be pressed into place.

Unmolding the ice cream need not be an ordeal. If your mold has a flat bottom, it may be lined with a piece of waxed paper cut to shape. The mold, with or without this lining, is quickly dipped in warm—not hot—water, and then dried. A chilled serving plate, with or without a paper doily, is placed over the mold, and both the mold and the plate are inverted. If the ice cream does not slip out easily, the mold and the plate may be shaken gently. If the ice cream is quite firm, it will hold its shape well. Small imperfections may be dealt with by smoothing the ice cream with the side of a knife blade; and there are very few catastrophes which cannot be hidden under whipped cream. Ice cream, once unmolded onto its plate, can be kept in the freezer for an hour or two. The chilled plate and the paper doily (Mrs. Marshall's "dish paper") will help prevent skidding: cold ice cream on a room-temperature plate can achieve a remarkable degree of mobility. Pleated paper soufflé cases, which are now sometimes sold as nut cups, and their porcelain replicas may also be used for individual servings. Champagne glasses of the broad shallow type are excellent for serving sorbets.

Simple decorations can be made quickly; crystallized flowers and mint leaves can be put on in seconds, and whipped cream put through a fluted pastry tube takes very little more time. A sprinkling of chopped nuts is often attractive; the green of pistachio is especially good with whipped cream on any of the strawberry ices.

Nineteenth-century presentations were often very elaborate. Mrs. Marshall's *Fancy Ices* deals with them at great length. Take, for example, the "Princess Christian Timbale." A truncated cone of orange cake, hollow in the center, is covered with a maraschino icing. The center is filled with alternate layers of pistachio, strawberry, and maraschino ice cream; this ensemble is then set on a base of nougat and sprinkled with pistachio nuts and crystallized rose petals. Whenever such ice-cream-and-cake combinations are made, it is of the utmost importance that the cake be frozen until it is as cold as the ice cream. Then, shortly before serving, it may be moved from the freezer to the refrigerator.

Spun sugar was a favorite nineteenth-century ornament, and Mrs. Marshall's recipe, which follows, is still practical, though half the quantity is more than ample. When the syrup is the color of light honey it will spin readily. A fork with widely spaced tines works well. If the sugar is spun very fine it will be delicate and pliable, but when thickly spun it is like needles and can inflict a painful cut. Practice until you can spin it fine; discard any that is not. It is easier to spin sugar on a dry day, because sugar is very sensitive to

Spinning Sugar

damp and will not spin so well in a humid room. Spun sugar must be made within a few hours of use, and kept in a very dry place. Once spun, it can be cut with scissors. Swathed around a molded ice it makes a handsome silvery wreath.

Put half a pound of water [1 cup water] and one pound of Marshall's Cane Sugar [2¼ cups granulated sugar] into a clean copper sugar boiler or thick stewpan, cover the pan over, bring the contents to the boil, remove any scum as it rises from time to time, and continue boiling until the liquid forms a thick bubbled appearance (commonly called the crack); then take a small portion on a clean knife or spoon and plunge it immediately into cold water, and if it is then quite brittle and leaves the knife or spoon quite clear it is ready for spinning. If it clings or is at all soft or pliable continue the boiling until as above. When ready, take a small portion on a fork or spoon and rapidly throw it to and fro over a slightly-oiled rolling pin; continue until sufficient threads of sugar are obtained.

The use, with Mrs. Marshall's "American" sorbet, of imitation glasses made of frozen ice water, is an attractive conceit. Why American? Throughout the nineteenth century, New Englanders had cannily been exporting ice to Europe, the Caribbean, and even Asia. Several New England fortunes had been founded on ice. Thoreau has described how a work force of some hundred men cut ice from Walden Pond, looking just like farmers harvesting a crop, with teams of horses and sleds. They cut as much as a thousand tons of ice in one day from an acre of the pond's surface. It was for export, so that he could write "that the sweltering inhabitants of Charleston and New Orleans, of Madras and Bombay and Calcutta, drink at my well." Although mechanical freezing was common by the end of the century, ice remained fixed in the European mind as an especially American commodity, a notion that was reinforced in the case of ice cream by the American origin of the crank freezer. Mrs. Marshall calls her sorbet glasses American, though, because they were first used in the United States. A variety of ices in frozen containers was described by Ranhofer in *The Epicurean*. Among the celebrated visitors to New York to be honored by a banquet at Delmonico's was Charles Dickens. The gargantuan meal served him in 1867 had a *sorbet à l'américaine* for its mid-dinner respite. Ranhofer's recipe for it describes the use of glasses of ice, made from two-piece molds. In them he serves a lemon and orange sorbet enhanced with American champagne, kirsch, and prunelle. Dishes that self-destruct are a labor-saving device we should invent again. Mrs. Marshall gives further information about these ice cups:

The sorbet à l'américaine is peculiarly interesting, as it was first served in the cups or glasses formed of raw ice prepared in moulds in imitation of wine-glasses or cups. Its flavouring, when prepared in New York, is the sparkling Californian wine, Catawba, for which champagne is generally substituted in Europe. The moulds for making these ice cups or glasses consist of two parts, an inner and an outer cup, so that when fixed together they have the appearance of one cup; but between the two parts is a space which is filled with pure or coloured water. These are set in the ice-cave till the water is frozen; the ice-cups are then turned out of the moulds and used. The pretty effects which can be produced by real ice-glasses prepared in this way are so numerous that these moulds are now being used for sorbets of any kind.

The most famous source of Catawba wine was in the Ohio River valley where horti-culturist Nicholas Longworth experimented with a variety of grapes. He sent a gift of some of his Catawba wine to Henry Wadsworth Longfellow, who was inspired to reply in verse and at length; the following stanzas are a sample:

> The richest and best
> Is the Wine of the West
> That grows by the beautiful river,
> Whose sweet perfume
> Fills all the room
> With a benison on the giver.

> Very good, in its way,
> Is the Verzenay,
> Or the Sillery, soft and creamy;
> But Catawba Wine
> Has a taste more divine—
> More dulcet, delicious, and dreamy.

More than half of the recipes in *The Book of Ices* have been tested, including examples of all the basic kinds and all the more improbable ones. The recipes were followed exactly whenever possible. The reader will see that I have reduced the number of egg yolks called for. This is because our eggs are larger; in 1885 ten eggs weighed a pound, while ten USDA-graded "medium" eggs weigh slightly more. Generally speaking, my family and friends who resolutely tasted their way through more than sixty-five varieties of ice cream were enthusiastic as well as open-minded. The only varieties that no one liked were the curried soufflés à la Ripon, and the spinach cream ice. Of the latter, my son said that it was not bad, but he would rather not eat an entire teaspoonful. The rice cream ice led to argument; whether people liked it or not depended on childhood attitudes to rice pudding. It did have a rather flannelly texture. Reactions to the cucumber ice were strong and diverse. Two people who described themselves as not liking ice cream were pleased by it; the improving effect of a little chopped fresh mint was suggested. There was also disagreement about the brown-bread cream ice; it would do well, I think, as a lining for a bombe. When these curiosities are set aside, the picture becomes more uniform. The strawberry and vanilla bombe and the ginger bombe were especially well liked; so were the Nesselrode pudding and the coffee mousse, to which I added a little cognac. The white coffee cream ice, made with the "Very Rich" custard base, was wonderful. So, in a quite different way, were the ices. I think that our lemons, like our eggs, may be larger than Mrs. Marshall's were, because the lemon water ice, when made with six lemons, was really very intense; one diner compared eating it to licking a styptic pencil. When made with four lemons it was delicious. The orange ice was perfect; it bears no resemblance to commercial ices, being fresh and intense and not too sweet. The apple, pear, and cranberry ices were very good. The elderflower was pleasant, if odd; all the strawberry ices and ice creams were wonderful—the plain ice, the mousse, the sorbet, and the plombière—and each had its own special character. The tea mousse was thought insipid. Really strong coffee must be used in making the coffee mousse and soufflé.

Even the simplest mixtures, the plain cream ice and water ice flavored with fruit syrup, were good. They take only a minute to prepare, especially with the ice-cream machine that goes into the food freezer. When made with some home-bottled blackberry syrup from a friend's garden, they were delicious. Even commercial syrup, of good quality and with real flavorings, yielded water ices that children ate almost as quickly as they could be made.

The question of how much each recipe yields is difficult to answer, because the design of an ice-cream freezer affects how much air is beaten into the mixture as it freezes. In general, I found that basic ice waters and creams yielded about one quart when frozen. When crushed fruit or other bulky ingredients were added, the quantity was proportionally larger. The cook should feel entirely free to double or halve any of these recipes to suit the needs of a particular occasion.

In some of the recipes based on custard (Numbers 1-4), there is an anomaly: a pint of custard (2½ cups) is called for, although in practice the base recipes begin with a pint of liquid, to which other ingredients are subsequently added. In testing these recipes, I used the full quantity produced from the recipes as written, and the results were entirely satisfactory.

THE BOOK OF ICES.

INCLUDING

CREAM AND WATER ICES,
SORBETS, MOUSSES, ICED SOUFFLÉS, AND
VARIOUS ICED DISHES,

WITH

NAMES IN FRENCH AND ENGLISH,

AND

VARIOUS COLOURED DESIGNS FOR ICES.

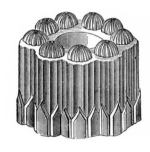

BY

A. B. MARSHALL.

(Copyright.)

LONDON:

MARSHALL'S SCHOOL OF COOKERY,

30, MORTIMER STREET, CAVENDISH SQUARE, W.

ESTABLISHED 1857.

[*Price Half-a-Crown.*]

A WORD ABOUT

MEASUREMENTS

THESE conversions are approximate. Precise measures were little used in the late-nineteenth-century kitchen. We level off our spoons when measuring dry ingredients; the English cook rounds them, often so generously that there is as much above the spoon as in it. Fortunately, the ounce remains constant, at twenty-eight grams, and the teaspoon is the same in both countries, though three of them make an American tablespoon and four go into a British one. Mrs. Marshall's "glasses" may mean anything she wants them to. Sources contemporary with her speak of a sherry wineglass as measuring one ounce, and the port wineglass as containing five ounces. *Whitaker's Almanack* (1894) says a wineglass measures two ounces. In the absence of any guidance from Mrs. Marshall, use a glass suitable to the liquid being measured: a liqueur glass for kirsch, a sherry glass for sherry, and so forth.

B. K. W.

CONTENTS.

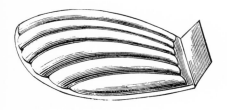

APPENDIX.

THE BOOK OF ICES

HINTS ON MAKING ICES.

1. Too much sugar will prevent the ice from freezing properly.

2. Too little sugar will cause the ice to freeze hard and rocky.

3. If the ices are to be moulded, freeze them in the freezer to the consistency of a thick batter before putting them in the moulds.

4. If they are to be served unmoulded, freeze them drier and firmer.

5. Broken ice alone is not sufficient to freeze or mould the ices ; rough ice and salt must be used.

8 parts crushed ice to 1 part rock salt.

6. Fruit ices will require to be coloured according to the fruit.   For Harmless Colours see p. 63.

7. When dishing up ices, whether in a pile or moulded, it will be found advantageous to dish them

B

on a napkin, as that will not conduct the heat to the bottom of them so quickly as the dish would.

Those who wish to be proficient can save themselves a great amount of time, trouble, and anxiety, as well as expense of materials, by attending at Marshall's School of Cookery on any day arranged for "Ices," when they will see the whole system in different branches practically taught, and be able to work from any recipes with ease.

FREEZING THE ICES.

See Introduction, pp. xxii–xxv.

Having prepared the cream, custard, or water ice as explained in the following recipes, take the Patent

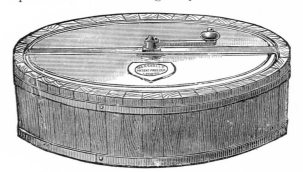

Freezer and lift the pan from the tub; put pounded ice in the tub to the depth of about 1 to $1\frac{1}{2}$ inch, according to the quantity of cream, etc., to be frozen, and throw over the pounded ice half its weight of freezing or rough salt and mix it in with the pounded ice. Replace the pan on the pivot in the tub; pour your cream, etc., into the pan through the little door in the lid and turn the handle. Observe, there is no need to pack ice and salt *round* the pan, but merely to put it on the bottom of the tub under the pan. After turning the handle for 2 or 3 minutes, examine the

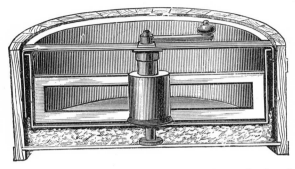

progress of the freezing by looking through the door in the lid. When the cream is sufficiently frozen (see Hints 3 and 4, p. 1), hold the pan with one hand and unscrew the handle and lift off the crossbar and lid.

Keep the freezer clean, and when cleaning take out the mixing fan.

N.B.—The cream, etc., in the pan should never be more than 1 inch deep. The shallower the layer is in the pan the quicker it will freeze.

For description, sizes, and prices of freezers, see p. 56.

MOULDING AND KEEPING ICES.

Take a patent cave and remove the lids as shown in the annexed engraving, and fill in between the metals with a mixture of 2 parts broken ice and 1 part salt; shake it well down so that the mixture goes underneath the cupboard of the cave, and fill well up

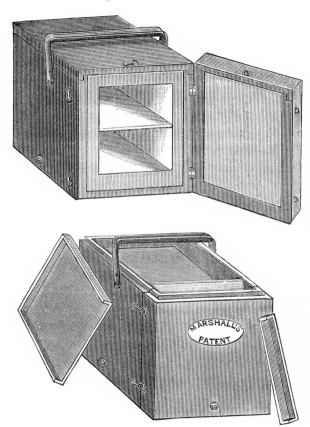

so that the lid will just slide over the ice and salt. Replace the lids.

Now fill your mould with the frozen cream from the freezer, and see that it is well pressed or shaken into the mould. Place the mould for $1\frac{1}{2}$ to 2 hours in the cave; examine from time to time if you wish. When you desire to turn the ice out of the mould, dip the mould for an instant in cold water and turn it out as you would a jelly. If you put the ice, when turned out, back into the cave and shut the door, it will keep its shape for many hours, so that ices can be prepared long before actually required; they have thus been kept from one day to another. When anything is freezing in the cave, do not open the door more often than necessary.

When the cave is done with, remove the brine and wash out with boiling water, and see that it is put away dry.

For description, sizes, and prices of caves, see p. 57.

THE SACCHAROMETER.

This is an instrument for testing quantity of sugar in water ices, etc. To ensure uniform success, it is necessary that the strength of the syrups should always be the same. Instructions for using the instruments are sent with them (see p. 63). Their use is strongly recommended.

The saccharometer, which measures the density of sugar syrup, is not used in any recipe in this book.

ICE MOULDS AND MOULDING.

These are to be had in almost endless variety—a list of some popular ones with prices will be found on pages 45–54.

In using ice moulds, great taste and novelty can be exercised in dishing up, and they afford to the cook the opportunity of making some of the prettiest dishes it is possible to send to the table.

Various coloured designs are given as examples in the body of this book.

CUSTARDS FOR CREAM ICES.

Never allow the *custard to boil,* or it will curdle.

Always add the flavouring when the custard is cooled, unless otherwise stated.

1.—Very Rich.

2½ cups cream
½ cup sugar
After boiling, cool cream slightly.
7 egg yolks
Optional: 1¼ cups whipped cream

1 pint of cream, a quarter of a pound of castor sugar, and 8 yolks of eggs.

Put the cream in a pan over the fire, and let it come to the boil, and then pour it on to the sugar and yolks in a basin and mix well. Return it to the pan and keep it stirred over the fire till it thickens and clings well to the spoon, but do not let it boil; then pass it through a tammy, or hair sieve, or strainer. Let it cool; add vanilla or other flavour, and freeze. Mould if desired. When partly frozen, half a pint of whipped cream slightly sweetened may be added to each pint of custard.

2.—Ordinary.

2½ cups milk or milk and cream
½ cup sugar
After boiling, cool milk slightly.
7 egg yolks

1 pint of milk, a quarter of a pound of castor sugar, and 8 yolks of eggs. Prepare this as in the above

recipe. Flavour and freeze. This can be improved by using half a pint of milk and half a pint of cream instead of all milk.

3.—Common.

1 pint of milk, a quarter of a pound of sugar, and 2 whisked eggs. Put these in a pan and stir over the fire to *nearly* boiling. Remove it from the fire and stir in a quarter of an ounce of finest leaf gelatine (see p. 64). When the gelatine is dissolved, pass it through the tammy, or hair sieve, or strainer. Flavour and freeze as above.

2¼ cups milk
½ cup sugar
2 eggs, well beaten
½ Tb powdered gelatin soaked
      5 minutes in ¼ cup cold milk

4.—Cheap.

1 pint of milk, a quarter of a pound of sugar, half an ounce of corn flour or arrowroot, etc. Boil the corn flour in the milk with the sugar. Finish as for the other custards.

2½ cups milk
½ cup sugar
3¾ tsp cornstarch or 2½ tsp arrowroot

5.—PLAIN CREAM ICE (*Crème Glacée*).

1 pint of cream sweetened with a quarter of a pound of castor sugar. Freeze dry.

This can be served in the centre of a compote of fruits, or with fresh fruits arranged round it; or the fruits and the cream can be served on separate dishes.

2½ cups cream
½ cup sugar

6.—CREAM ICES MADE FROM JAMS.

As jams vary exceedingly in the amount of sugar they contain, it is most necessary that this be taken into consideration to ensure success. The following recipe is for jams of average sweetness.

Boil 1 pint of milk and then mix it into 8 raw

2½ cups milk

After boiling, cool milk slightly.

7 egg yolks
½ cup plus 2 Tb jam
1¼ cups whipped cream sweetened
with ½ tsp sugar

½ cup plus 2 Tb jam
The juice of 1 lemon
2½ cups cream

Unsweetened custard (Nos. 1-4)
⅓ cup fruit syrup

⅓ cup fruit syrup
1¼ cups cream or milk

yolks of eggs, put this in a pan and stir over the fire until it thickens, then add a teacupful of jam and pass through the tammy or hair sieve. When cool freeze, and when partly frozen add half a pint of whipped cream sweetened with half a teaspoonful of castor sugar. Colour the custard with a little red, green, or yellow colour (p. 63) according to fruit.

7.—Another way.

Take a teacupful of jam as above, and the juice of 1 lemon and 1 pint of cream; pass through the tammy or sieve, and freeze. Colour according to fruit.

8.—CREAM ICES MADE FROM FRUIT AND LIQUEUR SYRUPS.

The syrups made by different manufacturers vary much in strength. The following recipe is for the syrups mentioned on p. 62.

Make a custard as in Nos. 1, 2, 3, or 4, without sugar, and add 4 tablespoonfuls of syrup to half a pint of custard, and freeze. Mould or serve in a pile.

9.—Another way: very simple.

Add 4 tablespoonfuls of fruit or liqueur syrup to half a pint of cream or milk. Freeze. Mould or serve in a pile.

CREAM ICES MADE FROM RIPE FRUITS, ETC.

10.—Almond or Orgeat Cream Ice (*Crème d'Amandes* *).

Blanch, peel, and pound half a pound of sweet almonds mixed with 6 or 7 bitter ones. During the pounding add a teaspoonful of orange flower water and 3 or 4 drops of essence of almonds, and a pint of tepid milk or cream (or half milk and half cream). Sweeten with 4 ounces of sugar, and add to 1 pint of custard (Nos. 1 to 4) or 1 pint of sweetened cream (No. 5). Freeze and serve in a pile on a napkin or mould it.

½ lb. almonds
Pound: Purée in blender or
    food processor.
3 or 4 drops bitter-almond flavoring
    or ⅛ tsp almond extract
1 tsp orange-flower water
2½ cups tepid milk or cream
½ cup sugar
2½ cups custard (Nos. 1-4) or cream
    (No. 5)

11.—Apple Cream Ice (*Crème de Pommes*).

Peel and cut up 2 pounds of apples, put them on the stove in half a pint of water, a little piece of cinnamon, the peel of half a lemon, the juice of one, and 6 ounces of sugar. Cook quickly until reduced to a purée, then pass through the tammy cloth or hair sieve, and mix it with 1 pint of sweetened cream (No 5) or 1 pint of custard (Nos. 1 to 4). Freeze and serve as for previous recipe.

2 lbs. apples
1¼ cups water
A ½-inch cinnamon stick
The peel of ½ lemon
The juice of 1 lemon
¾ cup sugar
Tammy cloth: Use a food mill.
2½ cups custard (Nos. 1-4) or cream
    (No. 5)

12.—Apricot Cream Ice (*Crème d'Abricots*).

Cut 12 apricots in halves, crack the stones and take out the kernels, and put them to cook with half

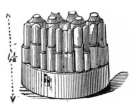

* The French names can be written in either of the following forms, as for Vanilla Cream Ice:—Crème à la Vanille, Crème de Vanille and the word " glacée " may be added; or Glace à la Vanille.

12 apricots

Crack the stones: See Glossary.

½ cup sugar

1¼ cups water

3 or 4 drops bitter-almond flavoring
or ⅛ tsp almond extract

½ tsp vanilla

3¾ cups custard (Nos. 1-4, increased
by half) or cream (No. 5,
increased by half)

6 ripe bananas

Pound: Purée in blender, food mill,
or food processor.

The juice of 2 lemons

2 Tb curaçoa

2½ cups cream (No. 5) or custard
(Nos. 1-4)

Biscuit: See Glossary.

2½ cups biscuit crumbs

1 lb. black currants

¾ cup sugar

1¼ cups water

2½ cups custard (Nos. 1-4) or cream
(No. 5)

¼ tsp lemon juice

a pint of water and 4 ounces of sugar. When tender mix a little liquid saffron or apricot yellow (p. 63) with the fruit and a few drops of vanilla, and pass through the tammy cloth or hair sieve. Add this purée to 1½ pints of custard (Nos. 1 to 4) or to the sweetened cream (No. 5). Freeze and finish as for previous recipes.

13.—Banana Cream Ice (*Crème de Bananes*).

Peel 6 ripe bananas and pound them to a pulp, add the juice of 2 lemons and a glass of curaçoa (p. 62). Pass through the tammy cloth and finish with 1 pint of sweetened cream or custard as in previous recipe.

14.—Biscuit Cream Ice (*Biscuits glacés à la Crème*).

This ice can be made with the pieces of any kind of biscuit ; rub them through the wire sieve and finish as for brown bread ice (No. 16).

15.—Black Currant Cream Ice (*Crème de Cassis*).

Put 1 pound of ripe black currants, 6 ounces of castor sugar, a tumblerful of water, and a few drops of carmine (p. 63) in a pan, and let them just come to the boil. Pass through the tammy and add 1 pint of custard (Nos. 1 to 4) or 1 pint of sweetened cream (No. 5), and 6 drops of lemon-juice. Freeze and finish as No. 10.

16.—Brown Bread Ice (*Crème de Pain Bis*).

Make a pint of brown bread crumbs and mix them with 8 tablespoonfuls of noyeau or maraschino syrup (p. 62) and 1 pint of cream or milk, and freeze dry. Serve in a pile or mould. This is a good entremet or dessert ice, and is much liked for garden and evening parties.

2½ cups brown bread crumbs
A scant ⅔ cup crème de noyeau
   or maraschino
2½ cups cream or milk

17.—Burnt Almond Cream Ice (*Crème de Pralines*).

Blanch and peel the almonds as in No. 10; put them in a sauté pan with an ounce of fresh butter and an ounce of castor sugar, and fry till a dark brown colour. Then pound in the mortar till smooth, adding by degrees 1 pint of hot milk or cream sweetened with three ounces of sugar, and 3 or 4 drops of essence of almonds. Pass through the tammy or hair sieve. Freeze and finish as in No. 10.

½ lb. almonds
2 Tb butter
2 Tb sugar
Pound: Chop very fine in blender
   or food processor.
2½ cups hot milk or cream
⅓ cup sugar
⅛ tsp almond extract

18.—Cedrat Cream Ice (*Crème à la Cédrat*).

Take one or two cedratti and rub them well with four or five large lumps of sugar, and add these lumps to a quart of lemon cream ice, and freeze. Serve rough or mould.

Cedrat: See Glossary.
For cedratti, substitute ¼ cup finely
   diced citron.
4 or 5 lumps sugar
5 cups lemon cream ice (No. 36)

19.—Cherry Cream Ice (*Crème de Cerises*).

Stone 1 pound of cherries, break the stones and take out the kernels, and cook the cherries and kernels

1 lb. cherries

Break the stones: See Glossary.

1¼ cups water

⅛ tsp almond extract or 3 drops
    bitter-almond flavoring

⅓ cup sugar

Pound: Purée in blender, food mill,
    or food processor.

The juice of 1½ lemons

2½ cups custard (Nos. 1-4) or cream
    (No. 5)

2 Tb kirsch

Pass 1½ lbs. warm roasted and cleaned
    chestnuts through a food mill.

½ tsp vanilla

⅓ cup sugar

2½ cups tepid cream

Optional: 2½ cups custard (Nos. 1-4)
    or cream (No. 5)

4 ounces semisweet chocolate

½ cup plus 2 Tb milk or cold water

2½ cups custard (Nos. 1-4) or cream
    (No. 5)

Optional: Dutch process cocoa, 1 Tb
    per 2½ cups custard

for about 10 minutes in half a pint of water and 3 ounces of castor sugar ; then pound them, and add the juice of 1½ lemons, and a little carmine or cherry red to colour (p. 63). Pass through a tammy cloth or hair sieve, and add to a pint of custard (Nos. 1 to 4) or sweetened cream (No. 5) and a wine-glass of kirsch, and freeze. Serve in a pile on a napkin or mould.

20.—Chestnut Cream Ice (*Crème de Marrons*).

Roast a quart of chestnuts, and when fully softened remove all husk and skin and pound them in a mortar, adding during the pounding by degrees a few drops of essence of vanilla, 3 ounces of castor sugar, a pint of tepid cream, and 6 drops of carmine (p. 63). When well mixed pass through hair sieve or tammy cloth. This may be frozen as it is, or added to a pint of custard (Nos. 1 to 4) or sweetened cream (No. 5), and finished as in previous recipes.

21.—Chocolate Cream Ice (*Crème de Chocolat*).

Cut a quarter of a pound of vanilla chocolate very fine, and put it in a quarter of a pint of milk or cold water on the stove to cook till quite dissolved ; then add this to 1 pint of custard (Nos. 1 to 4) or 1 pint of sweetened cream (No. 5). Freeze and finish as for vanilla cream ice (No. 58).

Cocoa cream ice may be made by adding 2 teaspoonfuls of Bensdorf soluble cocoa to 1 pint of custard, and finished as usual.

22.—Cinnamon Cream Ice (*Crème de Cannelle*).

Put 1 pint of milk or cream to boil with a finger-length of cinnamon, 1 bay leaf, and the peel of half a lemon; when well flavoured, mix it on to 8 raw yolks of eggs and 4 ounces of castor sugar; thicken over the fire. Add a little apricot yellow (p. 63); tammy, and finish as for other ices.

2½ cups milk or cream
A ¾-inch cinnamon stick
1 bay leaf
The peel of ½ lemon
Cool liquid slightly.
7 egg yolks
½ cup sugar

23.—Cocoanut Cream Ice (*Crème de Noix de Coco*).

Grate a small cocoanut, and stir this with 1 quart of custard just as you take the latter from the fire. Strain through tammy or hair sieve. Freeze and mould as before.

1 coconut: See Glossary.
5 cups custard (Nos. 1-4, doubled)

24.—Coffee Cream Ice (*Crème de Café*).

Make 1 pint of strong coffee (coffee extract is sometimes used), sweeten with 3 ounces of sugar; add this to 1 quart of custard (p. 6.) Freeze and finish as above. This ice will be brown, and not so delicate as the following.

2½ cups strong coffee
⅓ cup sugar
5 cups custard (Nos. 1-4, doubled)

25.—White Coffee Cream Ice : very delicate (*Crème de Café blanche*).

Take a quarter of a pound of fresh roasted Mocha coffee berries, and add them to a pint of cream or milk; let them stand on the stove for an hour, but do not let them boil; strain through tammy; sweeten with 3 ounces of sugar. Freeze and finish as for vanilla cream ice (No. 58).

¼ lb. mocha beans
2½ cups cream
Heat over low flame.
⅓ cup sugar
2½ cups custard (Nos. 1-4)
1 tsp vanilla
1 cup plus 2 Tb whipped cream

26.—Cranberry Cream Ice (*Crème de Cranberges*).

1 lb. cranberries
¾ cup sugar
1¼ cups water
2½ cups cream (No. 5) or custard
    (Nos. 1-4)
1 Tb maraschino

Put 1 pound of cranberries in a pan with 6 ounces of sugar, a few drops of carmine (p. 63), and half a pint of water. Cook until a pulp, then pass through the tammy, and add 1 pint of sweetened cream (No. 5) or custard (Nos. 1 to 4), and half a wine-glass of maraschino syrup. Freeze and finish as for previous ices.

27.—Cucumber Cream Ice (*Crème de Concombres*).

1 large cucumber
½ cup sugar
1¼ cups water
Pound: Purée in blender or food
    processor, or with finest grid of
    food mill.
2 Tb ginger brandy
The juice of 2 lemons
2½ cups cream (No. 5) or custard
    (Nos. 1-4)

Peel and remove the seeds from the cucumber, and to 1 large-sized cucumber add 4 ounces of sugar and half a pint of water; cook till tender. Then pound and add to it a wine-glass of ginger brandy and a little green colouring and the juice of two lemons; pass through the tammy, and add this to 1 pint of sweetened cream or custard. Freeze and finish as usual.

28.—Curaçoa Cream Ice (*Crème au Curaçoa*).

2½ cups unsweetened custard
    (Nos. 1-4) or unsweetened cream
    (No. 5)
The juice of 2 oranges
¼ cup curaçoa
3 Tb sugar

Take 1 pint of unsweetened custard (Nos. 1 to 4) or unsweetened cream; add the juice of 2 sweet oranges, 2 large wine-glasses of curaçoa or curaçoa syrup, and 1½ ounces of castor sugar. Freeze and mould or serve roughly.

29.—Damson Cream Ice (*Crème de Prunes de Damas*).

Put 1 pound of ripe damsons to cook with 6 ounces of castor sugar, with half a pint of water, a little liquid carmine; just boil up and then pass through the tammy. Add this to 1 pint of custard or cream (Nos. 1 to 5), and half a glass of noyeau syrup (p. 62), and freeze.

1 lb. damson plums
¾ cup sugar
1¼ cups water
2½ cups custard (Nos. 1-4) or cream (No. 5)
1 Tb crème de noyeau

30.—Filbert Cream Ice (*Crème d'Avelines*).

Shell and put 1 pint of filberts in a pan with cold water, and put to boil; when they boil strain off and wash in cold water and rub them in a cloth to take off the skins. When this is done, put the filberts in the mortar and pound them till quite smooth; then mix with them gently 8 raw yolks of eggs, 1 pint of cream, 4 ounces of castor sugar; put it into a pan and stir over the fire to thicken, keeping it stirred all the time; then pass through the tammy, and add a teaspoonful of essence of vanilla, and freeze.

2½ cups filberts
Cold water to cover
Pound: Grate in blender or
food processor.
7 egg yolks
2½ cups cream
½ cup sugar
1 tsp vanilla

31.—Ginger Cream Ice (*Crème au Gingembre*).

Pound half a pound of preserved ginger till smooth; then add to it 10 raw yolks of eggs, 3 ounces of sugar, 1½ pints of cream, and 1 glass of ginger wine; thicken it over the fire, then tammy and freeze.

½ lb. preserved ginger
8 egg yolks
⅓ cup sugar
3¾ cups cream
¼ cup ginger wine

32.—Gooseberry Cream Ice (*Crème de Groseilles Vertes*).

Put 1 quart of gooseberries on the stove in a pan, with half a pint of water, 6 ounces of sugar; boil, and when cooked pass through the tammy. If green berries, use a little sap green, or apple green (p. 63),

5 cups gooseberries
1¼ cups water
¾ cup sugar
2½ cups cream (No. 5) or custard (Nos. 1-4)

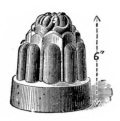

6"

5 cups ripe greengage plums
1¼ cups water
1¼ cups sugar
2 Tb maraschino
Tammy: Use blender, food mill, or
    food processor.
5 cups custard (Nos. 1-4, doubled) or
    cream (No. 5, doubled)

3¾ cups cream or milk
The peel of ¼ lemon
A 1-inch cinnamon stick
Cool liquid slightly.
8 egg yolks
¾ cup sugar
2 Tb brandy
1 Tb crème de noyeau
The juice of 1 lemon

3¾ cups cream (No. 5, increased by
    half) or custard (Nos. 1-4,
    increased by half)
⅓ cup kirsch
2 Tb brandy
The juice of 1 orange or lemon

to colour ; if red, a little carmine or cherry red. When tammied, mix with a pint of sweetened cream or custard, and freeze.

33.—Greengage Cream Ice (*Crème de Prunes de Reine-Claude*).

Stone 2 pints of ripe greengages, put half a pint of water in a pan with 8 ounces of sugar, and boil the fruit till quite smooth ; then add a little green colouring, a wine-glassful of maraschino syrup, and pass through the tammy. Add this to 2 pints of custard or cream (Nos. 1 to 5), and finish as usual.

34.—Italian Cream Ice (*Crème à l'Italienne*).

Scald 1½ pints of cream or milk, with a little lemon peel and cinnamon, and mix it on to 10 raw yolks of eggs ; sweeten with 6 ounces of castor sugar ; thicken over the fire, tammy, and flavour, when cool, with a large wine-glassful of pale brandy, half a glass of noyeau, and the juice of 1 lemon. Freeze, and serve as in previous recipes.

35.—Kirsch Cream Ice (*Crème au Kirsch*).

To 1½ pints of sweetened cream or custard add 3 wine-glasses of kirsch syrup, 1 glass of pale brandy, and the juice of 1 orange or lemon. Freeze.

36.—Lemon Cream Ice (*Crème de Citron*).

Peel 6 lemons very thinly, and put this peel to boil, with 1¼ pints of cream or milk and 5 ounces of sugar, for 10 minutes; then mix on to 10 raw yolks of eggs, and thicken over the fire and pass through the tammy. When cool add the juice from the lemons, which must be strained, and freeze.

The peel of 4 to 6 lemons
3 cups plus 2 Tb cream or milk
⅔ cup sugar
Cool liquid slightly.
8 egg yolks
The juice of 4 to 6 lemons

37.—Marmalade, Orange or Lemon, Cream Ice (*Crème au Marmelade*).

Mix a teacupful of marmalade with 1 pint of cream or unsweetened custard and the juice of 2 of the fruit, either lemon or orange, and 1 wine-glassful of orange or lemon syrup. Pass through the tammy, and freeze.

½ cup plus 2 Tb marmalade
2½ cups cream or unsweetened custard (Nos. 1-4)
The juice of 2 lemons or oranges

38.—Maraschino Cream Ice (*Crème au Marasquin*).

To 1 pint of cream or unsweetened custard add 4 wine-glasses of maraschino or maraschino syrup and the juice of 1 lemon, and freeze.

2½ cups cream or unsweetened custard (Nos. 1-4)
½ cup maraschino
The juice of 1 lemon

39.—Neapolitan or Pinachée Cream Ices (*Petites Crèmes à la Napolitaine*).

You must have a Neapolitan box for this ice (p. 52), and fill it up in 3 or 4 layers with different coloured and flavoured ice creams (a water ice may be used with the custards); for instance, lemon, vanilla, chocolate,

Panachée: In variegated colors.
A small straight-sided loaf pan

c

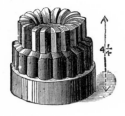

2½ cups cream
½ cup crème de noyeau
The juice of 1 orange
The juice of 1 lemon

4 ounces almonds

Pound: Chop very fine in blender
　　or food processor.

3 or 4 drops bitter-almond flavoring or
　　⅛ tsp almond extract
½ cup plus 2 Tb cream
¾ cup sugar
6 egg yolks
2½ cups cream
¼ cup orange-flower water
¼ tsp vanilla

and pistachio.　Mould in the patent ice cave for about 1½ to 2 hours, turn it out, cut it in slices, and arrange neatly on the dish on a napkin or dish-paper.

40.—Noyeau Cream Ice (*Crème au Noyeau*).

To 1 pint of cream add 4 glasses of noyeau or noyeau syrup, and the juice of 1 orange and 1 lemon. Freeze.

41.—Orange Cream Ice (*Crème à l'Orange*).

This is made as for lemon (No. 36), using oranges instead of lemons.

42.—Orange Flower Water Cream Ice (*Crème à la Fleur d'Oranger*).

Blanch 4 ounces of sweet almonds and 6 bitter almonds; pound them in the mortar till quite smooth, then mix with a quarter of a pint of cream, 6 ounces of castor sugar, and 7 raw yolks of eggs; add, when this is mixed well, 1 pint of cream, and then thicken over the fire, and tammy.　When cool, add two wine-glasses of orange flower water, and a few drops of essence of vanilla, and freeze.

43.—Peach Cream Ice (*Crème de Pêches*).

This is made in the same manner as the apricot ice.　A *very* little carmine is used for the colour.

44.—Pear Cream Ice (*Crème de Poires*).

This is made in the same manner as the apple ice (No. 11).

45.—Pine-apple Cream Ice (*Crème d'Ananas*).

Peel off the outside of the pine-apple; if not fully ripe, it will require to be boiled. Put the pine-apple in a clean pan with 1 pint of water and half a pound of sugar, and cook till tender. Then pound, and pass through hair sieve or tammy. To half a pint of this purée add 1 pint of cream or custard (Nos. 1 to 5). Freeze. Colour the ice required for the body of the pine-apple mould with apricot yellow, and that for the top with a little apple green. Another way is to make a purée of the tinned pine-apple, and add it to the custard or cream (Nos. 1 to 5). See coloured plate.

1 pineapple
2½ cups water
1¼ cups sugar
Pound and pass through hair sieve: Purée in blender, food mill, or food processor.
2½ cups cream (No. 5) or custard (Nos. 1-4)
½ pint = 1¼ cups purée

46.—Pistachio Cream Ice (*Crème de Pistaches*).

Blanch, peel, and pound a quarter of a pound of pistachio kernels. Add, when thoroughly pounded, 2 tablespoonfuls of orange flower water, and 12 drops vanilla essence; pass through sieve or tammy, and add 1 pint of custard (Nos. 1 to 4). Colour with apple green or sap green (p. 63). Freeze and mould.

4 ounces pistachios
Pound: Chop very fine in blender or food processor.
A scant 3 Tb orange-flower water
1¼ tsp vanilla
2½ cups custard (Nos. 1-4)

47.—Plum Cream Ice (*Crème de Prunes*).

Put 2 pounds of plums in a pan with half a pint of water and half a pound of sugar and a few drops

2 lbs. plums
1¼ cups water
1¼ cups sugar
Tammy: Use food mill, blender, or
    food processor.
½ pint = 1¼ cups purée
2½ cups cream (No. 5) or custard
    (Nos. 1-4)
⅛ tsp almond extract

½ cup plus 2 Tb quince jam
The juice of 2 oranges
The juice of ½ lemon
3¾ cups cream or unsweetened custard
    (Nos. 1-4, increased by half)
3 Tb pineapple syrup

1 lb. raspberries
¾ cup sugar
The juice of 1 lemon
2½ cups custard (Nos. 1-4) or cream
    (No. 5)

Bruise: Pulverize.
Ratafia biscuits: See Glossary.

3¾ cups milk
8 egg yolks
¾ cup sugar
1 Tb crème de noyeau

of carmine ; cook till smooth, and pass through the tammy. To half a pint of this purée add 1 pint of cream or custard (Nos. 1 to 5). A few drops of essence of almonds will improve it. Freeze and mould or serve in a pile.

48.—Quince Cream Ice (*Crème de Coings*).

Take a teacupful of quince jam, and add to it the juice of 2 oranges and of half a lemon, 1½ pints of cream or custard (unsweetened), a little apricot yellow to colour, 2 tablespoonfuls of pine-apple syrup. Pass through the tammy, and freeze.

49.—Raspberry Cream Ice (*Crème de Framboises*).

Take 1 pound of raspberries, 6 ounces of sugar, and the juice of a lemon ; mix with one good pint of custard or cream (Nos. 1 to 5). Tammy, and colour with liquid carmine or cherry red (p. 63). Freeze, and finish as for other ices.

50.—Ratafia Cream Ice (*Crème au Ratafia*).

Bruise 1 pound of ratafia biscuits in the mortar. Make a custard (see Nos. 1 to 4) of 1½ pints of milk, 10 raw yolks, and 6 ounces of sugar ; and when it thickens, pour it over the bruised biscuits, and pass altogether through the tammy or hair sieve. Add half a wine-glass of noyeau syrup, and freeze.

51.—Red Currant Cream Ice (*Crème de Groseilles*).

Make this as for raspberry cream ice (No. 49).

52.—Rhubarb Cream Ice (*Crème de Rhubarbe*).

Make this as for gooseberry cream ice (No. 32), using good ripe rhubarb.

53.—Rice Cream Ice (*Crème de Riz*).

Put 1 pint of new milk or cream to boil with 4 ounces of castor sugar, the peel of a lemon, 3 bay leaves, and a little cinnamon. Then put 3 ounces of rice cream (*crème de riz*) or ground rice in a basin, and mix it into a smooth paste with cold milk, and add the boiled milk, and let the whole simmer for 10 minutes. Pass through the tammy, strainer, or sieve, and when cold add a few drops of essence of vanilla, and freeze. During the freezing add half a pint of slightly sweetened whipped cream. Mould or serve roughly.

2½ cups milk or cream
½ cup sugar
The peel of 1 lemon
3 bay leaves
A 2-inch cinnamon stick
⅓ cup plus 2 Tb Cream of Rice
¼ cup cold milk
½ tsp vanilla
1¼ cups whipped cream sweetened
with ½ tsp sugar

54.—Spanish Nut Cream Ice (*Crème de Noisettes*).

Break a pint of Spanish nuts and bake the kernels till crisp, then pound them till smooth, and add the raw yolks of 8 eggs, 5 ounces of castor sugar, and 1 pint of cream; put in a stew-pan and stir over the fire till it thickens, and then pass through the tammy cloth. When cool, add half a wine-glass of noyeau syrup and half a wine-glass of brandy. Freeze and mould or serve in glasses.

2½ cups filberts
Bake the kernels in a 300° oven
until crisp.
Pound: Chop very fine in blender
or food processor.
7 egg yolks
⅔ cup sugar
2½ cups cream
1 Tb crème de noyeau
1 Tb brandy

Spanish Nut Cream Ice. Another way.

2½ cups filberts
¼ cup sugar
4 tsp orange-flower water
Pound: Chop very fine in blender
    or food processor.

1¼ cups cream
2 Tb plus 2 tsp maraschino or
    crème de noyeau
2½ cups custard or cream (Nos. 1-5)

Put the kernels of a pint of Spanish nuts, with 2 ounces of castor sugar and a tablespoonful of orange flower water, in a sauté or stew pan, and toss over a quick fire until the kernels are quite brown; then pound in the mortar, and mix well with half a pint of cream, pass through tammy cloth or hair sieve; flavour with 2 tablespoonfuls of maraschino or noyeau syrup (p. 62). Add this to 1 pint of the prepared custard or cream (Nos. 1 to 5). Freeze and mould or serve rough.

55.—Strawberry Cream Ice (*Crème de Fraises*).

Make this as raspberry cream (No. 49).

56.—Tangarine Cream Ice (*Crème de Tangarines*).

12 tangerines
2½ cups boiling cream or milk
Cool liquid slightly.

7 egg yolks
½ cup sugar
Tammy: Use food mill.

2 Tb orange-flower water
2½ cups cream or custard (Nos. 1-5)

Peel 12 tangarine oranges; make a pulp of the insides. Put the peels in a pint of boiling cream or milk, and let it stand on the stove for a quarter of an hour, but do not let it boil; then mix this with 8 raw yolks and 4 ounces of sugar, and stir over the fire till it thickens; now add the orange pulp, colour with apricot yellow, and pass through the tammy or hair sieve; when cool, add a wine-glass of orange flower water, and freeze. This may be added to 1 pint of sweetened cream or custard (Nos. 1 to 5) before freezing.

57.—Tea Cream Ice (*Crème de Thé*).

Prepare a teacupful of very strong tea, sweetened with 2 tablespoonfuls of sugar, and add this to 1 pint of custard or cream (Nos. 1 to 5), and finish as for other ices.

½ cup plus 2 Tb strong tea
A scant 3 Tb sugar
2½ cups custard or cream (Nos. 1-5)

58.—Vanilla Cream Ice (*Crème de Vanille*).

Prepare a custard (Nos. 1 to 4) or take sweetened cream (No. 5) and flavour with vanilla essence. Freeze and mould or serve in glasses. This is much improved by adding, during the freezing, a quarter of a pint of whipped cream to each pint of cream or custard.

To flavour with vanilla pods cut them in strips, and let them boil with the milk or cream of your custard, keeping the pan covered.

2½ cups custard (Nos. 1-4) or cream (No. 5)
2 tsp vanilla or 1 or 2 vanilla beans
½ cup plus 2 Tb whipped cream

59.—Walnut Cream Ice (*Crème de Noix*).

Make this as for filbert cream ice (No. 30).

60.—White Wine Cream Ice (*Crème au Vin blanc*).

Prepare a custard (No. 1) with 10 raw yolks of eggs, 1 pint of cream, and 4 ounces of sugar. When cool, add 3 glasses of white wine, 1 ditto pine-apple syrup, and freeze. When frozen, mix in 6 ounces of finely cut preserved fruits of any kind you have, and mould if desired.

8 egg yolks
2½ cups cream
½ cup sugar
6 Tb white wine
2 Tb pineapple syrup
¾ cup preserved fruit

FRUIT SYRUPS.

N.B.—If the prepared syrups referred to in some

½ cup plus 2 Tb jam
2½ cups cold water
The juice of 1 lemon

1¼ cups water
5½ Tb fruit syrup

1 lb. apples
2½ cups water
The peel of ¼ lemon
A 1-inch cinnamon stick
The juice of 1 lemon
½ cup sugar
1 pint = 2½ cups purée
2½ additional cups water sweetened
    with ½ cup sugar

of the foregoing recipes cannot be got at the time required, recourse may be had to the syrup in recipe No. 87 for sweetening purposes.

WATER ICES.

61.—Water Ices made from Jams.

To a teacupful of jam add 1 pint of cold water, the juice of 1 lemon; colour according to the fruit; pass through the tammy, and freeze. See note to No. 6.

62.—Water Ices made from Fruit Syrups.

To half a pint of water add 4 tablespoonfuls of the syrup (p. 62). Colour according to the fruit, and freeze. See note to No. 8.

WATER AND PERFUMED ICES MADE FROM RIPE FRUITS, ETC.

63.—Apple Ice Water (*Eau de Pommes*).

Put 1 pound of apples to cook in a pint of water, with a little lemon-peel, cinnamon, and juice of 1 lemon and 4 ounces of sugar; when cooked, pass through the tammy, and add to 1 pint of the purée 1 pint of water sweetened with 4 ounces of sugar or 8 tablespoonfuls of syrup (No. 87). Freeze and serve in mould or roughly.

64.—Apricot Ice Water (*Eau d'Abricots*).

Take 12 apricots and stone them, break the stones and pound the kernels; put the apricots to cook in a

clean pan with 6 ounces of sugar, 1 pint of water, and cook them till quite smooth; add a little apricot yellow, pass through the tammy, and add 1 pint of this pulp to 1 pint of water sweetened with sugar as in No. 63, or use the syrup No. 87, 8 tablespoonfuls to the pint of water, and freeze.

12 apricots
Break the stones: See Glossary.
1 Tb crème de noyeau or ⅛ tsp
  almond extract
¾ cup sugar
2½ cups water
Tammy: Use blender, food mill, or
  food processor.
2½ additional cups water
½ cup sugar or ⅔ cup syrup (No. 87)

65.—Banana Ice Water (*Eau de Bananes*).

Peel 6 ripe bananas, pound them, and add 4 ounces of sugar, 1 pint of water, and the juice of 2 oranges, or lemons if preferred, a little banana essence if you have it; pass through tammy, and freeze.

6 ripe bananas
Pound: Purée in blender, food mill,
  or food processor.
½ cup sugar
2½ cups water
The juice of 2 oranges or lemons
Optional: ¼ tsp banana essence

66.—Bergamot Ice Water (*Eau de Bergamote*).

Prepare a lemon or orange ice water for this, and to 1 pint of it add 2 glasses of pale brandy and 6 drops of essence of bergamot.   Freeze dry.

2½ cups lemon or orange ice water
  (Nos. 75 or 79)
¼ cup brandy
¼ tsp orange extract

67.—Black Currant Ice Water (*Eau de Cassis*).

This is made in the same manner as the barberry ice water.

See Introduction, p. xvii.

68.—Cedrat Ice Water (*Eau de Cédrat*).

Prepare 1 quart lemon ice water (No. 75), rub off the zest of two fine cedratti with a piece of loaf sugar, add it to the lemon water, tammy or strain it, and freeze.

Cedrat: See Glossary.
5 cups lemon ice water
  (No. 75, doubled)
Substitute: ¼ cup minced citron
  or to taste.

2 lbs. sour cherries

Crack the stones: See Glossary.

½ Tb crème de noyeau or ⅛ tsp
    almond extract

5 cups boiling water

1¼ cups sugar

Tammy: Use blender, food mill, or
    food processor.

2 Tb kirsch

2 cups cranberries

1¼ cups sugar

1¼ cups water

The juice of 2 lemons

Tammy: Use blender, food mill, or
    food processor.

½ pint = 1¼ cups pulp

2½ additional cups water

1 quart damson plums

½ lb. crystallized ginger

5 cups orange ice water (No. 79,
    doubled)

Grape Ice Water: See Introduction,
    p. xvii.

2½ cups lemon ice water (No. 75)

2 Tb dried elderflower infused with
    ¼ cup boiling water

¼ cup sherry

69.—Cherry Ice Water (*Eau de Cerises*).

Stone 2 pounds of Kentish cherries, crack the stones and pound the kernels, pour 1 quart of boiling water on the fruit and kernels and half a pound of sugar; colour with carmine and let stand till cold, then pass through the tammy, and add a wine-glassful of kirsch, and freeze.

70.—Cranberry Ice Water (*Eau de Cranberges*).

Put half a pound of cranberries to cook with 8 ounces of sugar, and half a pint of water; when cooked, add the juice of 2 lemons, a little carmine, and pass through the tammy. Add half a pint of this pulp to 1 pint of water, and freeze.

71.—Damson Ice Water (*Eau de Prunes de Damas*).

Stone 1 quart of damsons and make in the same manner as cherry ice water (No. 70). Freeze either for fancy moulds or to serve rough.

72.—Ginger Ice Water (*Eau de Gingembre*).

Pound 8 ounces of preserved ginger, mix it with 1 quart of orange ice water (No. 79); pass it through the tammy, and freeze. Either mould or serve rough.

73.—Grape Ice Water (*Eau de Grappes*).

To 1 pint of lemon ice water (No. 75) add a large wine-glassful of elder flower water and 2 wine-glassfuls of sherry. Freeze and mould or serve rough.

74.—Jasmine Ice Water (*Eau de Jasmin*).

This is made in the same way as bergamot, only essence of jasmine is used instead of bergamot. Freeze for moulding or to serve rough.

Substitute 2 Tb jasmine tea infused with ¼ cup boiling water.

75.—Lemon Ice Water (*Eau de Citron*).

1 pint of boiling water poured on to the peel of 8 lemons, half a pound of loaf sugar; when cool, mix with the juice of 6 lemons; add 6 drops of lemon essence; tammy or strain through sieve, and freeze for moulding or for serving in glasses.

2½ cups boiling water
The peel of 6 to 8 lemons
1¼ cups sugar
The juice of 4 to 6 lemons
⅛ tsp lemon extract

76.—Mille Fruits Ice Water (*Eau de Mille Fruits*).

Prepare 1 quart of lemon ice; add to it when partly frozen half a pound of mixed fruits cut in square pieces; any kind of fruit left from dessert will do for this ice. Serve in mould or rough.

5 cups lemon ice water (No. 75, doubled)
1 cup diced assorted fruit

77.—Melon Ice Water (*Eau de Melon*).

Take off the skin of the ripe melon and pound the melon till smooth, then add half a pint of water, 3 ounces of sugar, the juice of 2 oranges or lemons, and 1 glass of curaçoa or maraschino syrup; add this to 1 pint of water, and freeze for moulding or to serve rough.

1 melon
Pound: Purée in blender, food mill, or food processor.
1¼ cups water
⅓ cup sugar
The juice of 2 oranges or lemons
2 Tb curaçoa or maraschino
2½ additional cups water

78.—Mulberry Ice Water (*Eau de Mûres*).

1 lb. mulberries
½ cup sugar
The juice of 1 lemon
2½ cups cold water

Pick and then pound 1 pound of mulberries; add to them 4 ounces of sugar, a little liquid carmine, juice of 1 lemon; pass through the tammy, then add to 1 pint of cold water, and freeze.   Serve as in previous recipes.

79.—Orange Ice Water (*Eau d'Oranges*).

Prepare this the same as for lemon ice water, only use oranges instead of lemons.

80.—Peach Ice Water (*Eau de Pêches*).

6 ripe peaches
Crack the stones: See Glossary.
½ Tb crème de noyeau or ⅛ tsp
    almond extract
2½ cups water
½ cup sugar
The juice of 1 lemon
Tammy: Use blender, food mill, or
    food processor.
2 Tb crème de noyeau
2 Tb orange-flower water

Peel 6 good peaches and crack the stones, and remove the kernels, which must be pounded; put in a stew-pan with 1 pint of water, 4 ounces of sugar, and juice of 1 lemon; cook the fruit for 15 minutes, then tammy, and add a wine-glassful of noyeau and 1 glass of orange flower water, a little carmine. Freeze.

81.—Pear Ice Water (*Eau de Poires*).

6 ripe pears
3¾ cups water
¾ cup sugar
The peel of ¼ lemon
A 1-inch cinnamon stick
Tammy: Use blender, food mill, or
    food processor.

Peel 6 good-sized pears and cut in slices, and put them to cook in 1½ pints of water with 6 ounces of sugar, a little lemon peel and cinnamon; add a little carmine when cooked; pass them through a tammy, and freeze.

82.—Pine-apple Ice Water (*Eau d'Ananas*).

Peel the pine and take out the cores, put it to cook for 15 minutes, with 1½ pints of water, 6 ounces of sugar, and the juice of 2 lemons and 1 orange, then pound ; mix the liquor in which it was cooked with it and pass through the tammy, and freeze. A few pieces of the pine-apple may be cut in rounds or dice shapes, and added to the frozen ice just before serving. Mould if wished.

1 pineapple
3¾ cups water
¾ cup sugar
The juice of 2 lemons
The juice of 1 orange
Pound: Purée in blender, food mill, or food processor.
Pineapple cut in fancy shapes

83.—Raspberry Ice Water (*Eau de Framboises*).

This is prepared the same as for strawberry ice water, only using raspberries instead of strawberries.

84.—Red Currant Ice Water (*Eau de Groseilles*).

Proceed as for black currant ice water, only use red currants instead of black. Freeze, and mould if wished.

85.—Rose Water Ice (*Eau de Roses*).

Take half a pound of fresh-gathered rose leaves, pour 1 pint of boiling water on them, with 4 ounces of sugar, and keep closely covered up ; then strain off and colour with a little liquid carmine, and freeze.

½ lb. unsprayed rose petals
2½ cups boiling water
½ cup sugar
Let stand 5 minutes.

86.—Strawberry Ice Water (*Eau de Fraises*).

Put the strawberries in the mortar and pound them, and to 1 pound add 6 ounces of castor sugar, the

1 lb. strawberries
Pound: Purée in blender, food mill, or food processor.
¾ cup sugar
The juice of 1 lemon
2½ cups water

juice of 1 lemon, a little liquid carmine; pass through the tammy, mix this to 1 pint of cold water, and freeze. Serve as in previous recipes.

87.—Syrup for Water Ices.

3¾ cups sugar
7½ cups cold water

Put 1½ pounds of loaf sugar in a clean pan to boil with 3 pints of cold water, keep well skimmed, reduce to half the quantity, and strain through the tammy or clean cloth. This will keep well. It may be used for sweetening the ices instead of the sugar.

SORBETS, ETC.

The Italian word *sorbetto*, meaning sherbet, shows the origin of these dishes. Their general character is that of a water ice mixed or flavoured with wine or spirits. They are served before the roast in glasses or fancy cups, and generally just enough frozen to be piled up in the glass, or they may be moulded in little shapes and served with or without fruit. The following recipes will be sufficient for guidance, and they can be varied according to desire.

88.—Sorbet of Peaches (*Sorbet de Pêches à la Portugaise*).

6 ripe peaches
¾ cup sugar
The juice of 2 oranges or 12 grapes
½ Tb crème de noyeau or ⅛ tsp almond extract
2½ cups cold water
2 Tb kirsch
Sliced peaches, chopped pistachios

Take 6 ripe peaches and peel them, and add to them 6 ounces of castor sugar, the juice of 2 oranges or 1 dozen grapes; crack the stones and pound the kernels and put to the fruit, and add to 1 pint of cold water; add about 6 drops of liquid carmine and half a salt-spoonful of apricot yellow, and tammy; then freeze, and when frozen add 1 wine-glassful of kirsch,

and serve with sliced fresh peaches and chopped pistachio nuts over.

89.—Sorbet of Strawberries (*Sorbet de Fraises*).

Take 1 pound of strawberries, and add to them 6 ounces of castor sugar and a little carmine, the juice of 1 lemon; pass through the tammy, and to this add 1 pint of water, and partly freeze; then add 1 wine-glassful of curaçoa (p. 62), half a glass of rum or brandy; continue the freezing, and serve in sorbet cups or glasses. If you have little strawberry moulds, you can put the sorbet in them, and freeze them for about half an hour in the cave. Serve with cut fresh fruits over, which have been flavoured by being tossed in a little brandy and castor sugar.

1 lb. strawberries
¾ cup sugar
The juice of 1 lemon
2½ cups water
2 Tb curaçoa or 1 Tb rum or brandy
Sliced strawberries with sugar and
    brandy

90.—Sorbet of Apricots (*Sorbet d'Abricots à la Moscovite*).

Take 4 tablespoonfuls of apricot jam, about a salt-spoonful of apricot yellow, 1 pint of cold water, pass through the tammy and freeze; then add 1 wine-glassful of maraschino (p. 62) and a half wine-glassful of rum or brandy; freeze firm, and serve with square pieces of apricots, cherries, and angelica. In summer-time fresh fruit can be used, when the fruit should be cut up and a little sugar sprinkled over it before serving. This is served in sorbet cups or glasses.

⅓ cup plus 1 tsp apricot jam
2½ cups cold water
2 Tb maraschino
1 Tb rum or brandy
Angelica: See Glossary.
Diced preserved or fresh fruit

91.—Roman Punch (*Punch à la Romaine*).

5 cups water
2½ cups sugar
The peel of 3 lemons
Cool before adding lemon juice.
The juice of 4 to 6 lemons
¼ cup dark rum

Boil 1 quart of water, and add to it 1 pound of sugar ; when quite boiling, pour it on to the peel of 3 lemons and the juice of 6 lemons ; cover over till cold, then strain through the tammy, and freeze ; when partly frozen, add 2 glasses of Jamaica rum, and serve in sorbet cups or in glasses.

92.—Another way.

5 cups lemon ice water (No. 75, doubled)
5 egg whites, stiffly beaten
A pinch of salt
½ cup sugar
2½ Tb brandy
1¼ cups champagne

Make 1 quart of lemon ice water ; when cold, have the whites of 5 eggs whipped stiff, with a tiny pinch of salt, then add 4 ounces of castor sugar, and partly freeze the lemon ice, and then mix to it the whipped egg, and continue freezing in the machine till smooth ; when smooth, add 1 large wine-glassful of brandy and a half-pint of champagne ; continue to freeze, and serve in sorbet cups or glasses.

93.—American Sorbet (*Sorbet à l'Americaine*).

Imitation glasses, Catawba wine:
See Introduction, pp. xxvii–xxviii.

Make some imitation glasses, by freezing water in the proper tin moulds prepared for the purpose, and make a sorbet as above, flavouring it with Catawba wine or champagne. Serve the sorbet in the imitation glasses. These imitation cups or glasses can be made transparent, marble-like, or coloured.

94.—Rum Sorbet (*Sorbet au Rhum*).

Prepare a lemon water ice, and when nearly frozen, flavour with 2 glasses of Jamaica rum to the pint of prepared ice.

¼ cup dark rum per 2½ cups prepared lemon water ice (No. 75)

MOUSSES.

These make excellent sweets, and are very much liked on account of their lightness. They are served as an entremet, sometimes for dessert. The following recipes will show the method of making them.

Mousses are frozen without stirring.

95.—Coffee Mousse (*Mousse au Café*).

12 yolks of eggs, 4 whites, 2 large tablespoonfuls of castor sugar, 2 large tablespoonfuls of strong coffee, also little coffee colouring or essence; whip over boiling water till warm, then take off and whip till cold, and add a teacupful of whipped cream; whip these well together. Put in a mould, and place in the cave to freeze for about 2½ hours. To turn out, dip the mould in cold water. Serve with dish-paper, or napkin on dish.

9 or 10 egg yolks
4 egg whites
3 or 4 Tb sugar
3 Tb coffee
¼ tsp coffee extract
Use very hot but not boiling water.
½ cup plus 2 Tb whipped cream

96.—Strawberry Mousse (*Mousse aux Fraises*).

Put 16 raw yolks of eggs into a pan, with 6 whites of eggs, 4 ounces of castor sugar, and a quarter of a pint of the pulp of fresh strawberries, 1 teaspoonful of essence of vanilla, a little of liquid carmine to colour;

12 egg yolks
4 or 5 egg whites
½ cup sugar
½ cup plus 2 Tb strawberry purée
1 tsp vanilla
Use very hot but not boiling water.
1¼ cups whipped cream

D

2½ Tb maraschino

10 egg yolks
3 or 4 egg whites
¼ cup sugar
2 tsp vanilla
Use very hot but not boiling water.
½ cup plus 2 Tb whipped cream

Soufflés are not stirred while freezing.

whip till warm over boiling water, then remove and whip till cold and thick, then add half a pint of whipped cream; whip these together, and put into any fancy mould, and freeze for about 2½ hours in the cave. Turn out and dish same as No. 95.

97.—Maraschino Mousse (*Mousse au Marasquin*).

This is made in the same manner as the Mousse à la Vanille, but instead of the vanilla essence add 1 good wine-glassful of maraschino for flavour.

98.—Vanilla Mousse (*Mousse à la Vanille*).

Put 12 yolks of eggs into a pan, with 4 whites and 2 ounces of castor sugar, half a tablespoonful of essence of vanilla; whip this over boiling water till warm, then remove the pan from the fire and continue whipping till cold and stiff, then add to this 1 teacupful of whipped cream; put into any kind of mould, and set in the ice cave for 2½ hours. Turn out same as No. 95.

ICED SOUFFLÉS.

These very much resemble the Mousses, but as they are served in dishes or cases, and the mousses are moulded, a slight difference is required in the ingredients and in the time for freezing. The following recipes will be sufficient for guidance.

99.—Coffee Soufflé (*Soufflé au Café*).

Take a soufflé dish and surround it inside with paper standing about 2 inches above the top, and put it into the charged cave to get cold.

Take and whip over boiling water 12 raw yolks of eggs, 6 whites, 4 large tablespoonfuls of very strong coffee, 4 ounces of castor sugar, until like a thick batter, then remove and continue the whipping on ice till the mixture is cold; to this quantity add 2 teacupfuls of whipped cream; pour this into the mould, letting it rise above the mould to near the top of the paper. Freeze in the cave for $2\frac{1}{2}$ hours, and serve in the mould with napkin round or in silver soufflé dish. Of course these quantities may be proportionately increased or diminished to suit the size of the mould.

10 egg yolks
5 egg whites
⅓ cup very strong coffee
½ cup sugar
Use very hot but not boiling water.
1¼ cups whipped cream

100.—Vanilla Soufflé (*Soufflé à la Vanille*).

Prepare the soufflé dish as in No. 99. Take 9 raw yolks of eggs, $4\frac{1}{2}$ whites, $2\frac{1}{2}$ tablespoonfuls of castor sugar, little vanilla essence; whip over boiling water, take off when rather warm and whip till cold and stiff, then add about $4\frac{1}{2}$ tablespoonfuls of lightly sweetened whipped cream. Finish as in No. 99.

8 egg yolks
4 egg whites
3½ Tb sugar
1 tsp vanilla
Use very hot but not boiling water.
⅓ cup whipped cream

101.—Strawberry Soufflé (*Soufflé de Fraises*).

Prepare a mousse as in No. 96, using about half as much more cream whipped, and finish as in last recipe.

A total of 2 cups whipped cream

Paper soufflé cases: See Introduction, p. xxv.
Coffee soufflé (No. 99)

Strawberry ice water (No. 86)
FOR THE VANILLA CUSTARD:
1¼ cups milk or cream
1 vanilla bean
3 Tb sugar
4 egg yolks
3 additional Tb sugar
¼ tsp brandy

102.—Coffee Soufflés in cases (*Petits Soufflés au Café*).

Take the little paper soufflé cases and fasten round each a strip of white paper, fixing it with sealing wax ; let the paper stand about 1½ inches above the top of the case. Prepare the soufflé mixture as in No. 99 ; fill the case and over it to nearly the edge of the paper surrounding it, and place them in the charged cave for 1½ hours ; when frozen sufficiently remove the paper and serve.

Any soufflé can be served in a similar manner. Fruit and vanilla soufflés would be improved in appearance by sprinkling a little coloured sugar over them.

DRESSED ICES, ETC.

It is impossible to give more than a few under this head, as the variety that can be made with the various moulds, flavours, etc., is almost unlimited ; but the mixtures which can be used will be found among the foregoing recipes, and some designs in colours are given in the book as examples, also a list of some moulds on pages 45 to 54.

103.—Strawberry and Vanilla Bombe (*Bombe à la Vanille et Fraises*).

Prepare 1 pint of strawberry ice water and freeze it quite dry, have a half-pint of vanilla custard prepared with half a pint of milk or cream boiled with a stick of vanilla pod, 1½ ounces of castor

sugar, and when flavoured sufficiently pour on to 4 raw yolks of eggs and thicken over the fire; then tammy and freeze, and add, when partly frozen, 3 tablespoonfuls of castor sugar and 6 drops of brandy; line a bombe mould with the strawberry water ice and fill up the centre with the vanilla custard, and freeze for 2 hours in the patent ice cave. To turn out, dip the mould in cold water and serve on a napkin.

104.—Bombe with Fruits (*Bombe aux Fruits*).

Take a bombe mould and line it with chocolate ice cream, then fill up the centre with vanilla cream ice mixed with a wine-glassful of kirsch, half a pint of whipped cream, and cut candied fruits which have been soaked in syrup. Freeze in cave for two hours, turn out as in last recipe, and serve on a dish-paper or napkin.

Chocolate ice cream (No. 21)
Vanilla cream ice (No. 58)
2 Tb kirsch
1¼ cups whipped cream
Candied fruit to taste

105.—Sovereign Bombe (*Bombe à la Souveraine*).

Line the sides and top of a bombe with a layer of almond ice cream, and fill up the interior with a tea mousse (see recipe No. 95 for coffee mousse).

Freeze in the cave for 2 to 3 hours according to size of mould; serve it on a border of sponge cake, and garnish the dish with the same cake cut in small fancy shapes.

Almond ice cream (No. 10)
Coffee or tea mousse (No. 95)
A border of sponge cake: A sponge cake baked in a flat ring mold.

3¾ cups cream
1¼ cups milk
10 egg yolks
⅛ tsp mixed spice:
    See Glossary or substitute ⅛ tsp
    allspice.
1¼ cups sugar
1 vanilla bean
2½ Tb brandy
2 Tb kirsch

106.—Plain Ice Pudding (*Pouding Glacé*).

To 1½ pints of good cream add half a pint of new milk; put it in a stew-pan with the raw yolks of 12 eggs, a pinch of mixed spice, half a pound of castor sugar, 1 split pod of vanilla; stir this over the fire till it thickens and presents a creamy appearance on the wooden spoon; then tammy, and when cool add a large wine-glassful of brandy and a wine-glassful of kirsch; freeze, and put into any mould and freeze in the cave for 2 hours.

107.—Nesselrode Pudding (*Pouding à la Nesselrode*).

This is prepared the same as No. 106, with the addition of various cut fruits being mixed with the custard before putting into the mould. If fresh or dried fruits are used, they should be soaked in a little liqueur or spirit and sprinkled with sugar before being mixed. Fruits preserved in syrups may simply be cut up and mixed.

108.—Sauce for above.

A sauce is sometimes served with the Nesselrode pudding, and is made by preparing a rich custard (No. 1) and flavouring it with vanilla or maraschino. Keep it on the ice and serve as cold as possible.

109.—Chateaubriand Bombe (*Bombe à la Chateaubriand*).

Prepare 1½ pints of vanilla custard (Nos. 1 to 4), put the milk to boil with 4½ ounces of castor sugar and 1 pod of vanilla split in shreds; let this come to the boil, and remain on the side of the stove in the pan covered up for about 15 minutes, not boiling; then mix it on to 12 raw yolks of eggs and thicken over the fire. Divide the custard into two parts; put to one part a few drops of essence of vanilla and 1 tablespoonful of orange flower water, and colour it with apple green to the colour of pistachio, and tammy; it is ready then to freeze, and when partly frozen put about 4 tablespoonfuls of whipped cream, sweetened with half a teaspoonful of castor sugar. Put 3 ounces of blanched sweet almonds in a sauté pan, with half an ounce of fresh butter and 1 ounce of castor sugar; make these quite a deep brown over the fire, and then pound them quickly in the mortar till smooth; mix them with the other part of vanilla custard, and pass through the tammy; when frozen, add cream as to the other part of the custard, and freeze. Arrange the two ices thus prepared in a fancy mould in layers, or the mould can be entirely lined with the green, and the centre filled with the brown ice. Freeze for 2 hours in the cave.

FOR THE VANILLA CUSTARD:
3¾ cups milk or cream
⅔ cup sugar
1 vanilla bean
Cool liquid slightly.
10 egg yolks

PART ONE:
½ tsp vanilla
4 tsp orange-flower water
A scant ⅓ cup whipped cream
     sweetened with ½ tsp sugar

PART TWO:
1 Tb butter
3 ounces almonds
2 Tb sugar

110.—Ginger Bombe (*Bombe au Gingembre*).

1¼ cups milk
The peel of 1 lemon
⅓ cup sugar
3 or 4 egg yolks
¼ tsp ginger
The juice of 1 lemon
¼ tsp vanilla
1¼ cups whipped cream sweetened
        with ½ tsp sugar
⅓ cup diced crystallized ginger

Prepare a custard made with half a pint of milk, boiled with 1 lemon-peel and 3 ounces of castor sugar; when the milk boils, mix it on to 4 raw yolks of eggs and as much ginger as will cover a threepenny piece, thicken over the fire and tammy, then add the juice of 1 lemon and 6 drops of vanilla essence, and when cool freeze; when partly frozen, add half a pint of whipped cream sweetened with a saltspoonful of castor sugar; line the bombe mould with this, and have 3 ounces of preserved ginger cut in dice and put in the centre; fill up with more custard, and freeze for 1½ hours in the cave. Turn out and serve on a napkin or dish-paper.

111.—Bartlett Pudding (*Pouding à la Bartlett*).

6 ripe Bartlett pears
2½ cups water
The juice of 2 lemons
¾ cup sugar
Reserve the pear syrup.
¼ cup diced candied pineapple
¼ cup diced glacé cherries
1¼ cups heavy cream
3 egg whites, stiffly beaten
¼ cup sugar caramelized with ½ cup
        water
Add boiling caramel to the stiffly
        beaten egg whites, while
        continuing to beat them.

Peel and cut up in thin slices 6 ripe Bartlett pears, cook them in 1 pint of water with the juice of 2 lemons, 6 ounces of sugar; when tender, drain them on a sieve and pass the fruit through a tammy or fine hair sieve; mix with this 2 ounces of pine-apple cut fine, 2 ounces of dried cherries, and half a pint of thick cream, and freeze; when partly frozen, have ready to mix with it the whipped whites of 3 eggs, to which have been added 2 ounces of sugar, cooked to caramel. For this, put the sugar to boil with a quarter of a pint of water, and when cooked mix it with the eggs and add to the frozen mixture, and continue the freezing,

and mould. The syrup from the pears must be used
for the sauce for serving round the pudding. Prepare
it as follows : Whip the white of 1 egg and mix it
with 2 tablespoonfuls of whipped cream, half a glass
of maraschino syrup (p. 62); add the pear syrup and
cool over ice. When the pudding is turned out, pour
the sauce over it and serve.

1 additional egg white
2½ Tb whipped cream
1 Tb maraschino
The reserved pear syrup

112.—Plombière of Strawberries (*Plombière de Fraises*).

Put 1 pint of thick cream in a pan with the raw
yolks of 12 eggs, a tiny pinch of mixed spice, and half
a pound of castor sugar ; stir together on the stove,
and when nearly boiling add to it 1 pint of the pulp
of fresh strawberries which has been passed through
the tammy cloth, a little carmine, half a teaspoonful of
essence of vanilla, and a wine-glass of brandy ; freeze
and mould, and leave in the ice cave for 2 hours ; then
dip in cold water, and turn out on a napkin or dish-
paper.

2½ cups heavy cream
10 egg yolks
⅛ tsp mixed spice:
    See Glossary.
1¼ cups sugar
2½ cups strawberry purée
½ tsp vanilla
2 Tb brandy

113.—Muscovite of Oranges (*Moscovite d'Oranges*).

Put half a pound of loaf sugar with the peel of 8 or
10 oranges, a quarter of an ounce of Marshall's gelatine, and pour over them 1 pint of boiling water and
a little saffron yellow ; let this stand till cool, then
mix the juice of the oranges to it and strain through
the tammy, and add a little maraschino or brandy to
flavour. Pour into a mould and freeze for about

1¼ cups sugar
The peel of 8 to 10 oranges
The juice of 8 to 10 oranges
½ Tb powdered gelatin soaked 5
    minutes in ¼ cup cold orange
    juice
2¼ cups boiling water
½ Tb maraschino or brandy
Optional: whipped cream sweetened
    and flavored to taste

2 cups strawberry purée
¾ cup sugar
2¼ cups warm water
½ Tb powdered gelatin soaked 5
    minutes in ¼ cup cold water
The juice of 1 lemon
½ Tb crème de noyeau
Optional: cream, strawberries with
    syrup

¼ cup grated Parmesan cheese
3 Tb grated Gruyère cheese
A speck of cayenne
1¼ cups whipped cream
⅔ cup aspic (p. 44)
Browned bread crumbs

2 hours in the cave; turn out as in the last recipe.
This can be served with whipped cream sweetened and
flavoured.

114.—Muscovite of Strawberries (*Moscovite de Fraises*).

Pass 1 pound of ripe strawberries through the
tammy, add 6 ounces of castor sugar, 1 pint of warm
water, in which has been dissolved a quarter of an ounce
of Marshall's finest leaf gelatine, the juice of 1 lemon,
a little carmine, and a little noyeau; pour into a mould,
and put to freeze for about 2 hours in the cave. To
turn it out, put the mould into cold water for a few
seconds. This can be served with cream or fresh
strawberries, mixed with a little syrup. Colour to
the fruit.

115.—Little Soufflés of Cheese (*Petits Soufflés de Fromage Glacés*).

Three tablespoonfuls of grated Parmesan cheese, 2
ditto of gruyère, little cayenne, half a pint of whipped
cream, and rather more than a quarter of a pint of
aspic jelly. Mix and fill up the cases (see No. 102),
and freeze in the cave for 1 hour. Serve with browned
bread-crumbs on the top.

116.—Iced Spinach à la Crème (*Epinards Glacées à la Crème*).

Put 2 or 3 handfuls of spinach in cold water with
salt, and a very tiny pinch of soda; let it come to the

boil; strain off and press the water from it. Boil half a pint of milk and stir it on to 4 yolks of eggs, and put it on the stove again to thicken—don't let it boil; add a little apple green to colour it, and to half a pint of the custard add a small dessert-spoonful of castor sugar and a pinch of salt; mix with the spinach, pass through the tammy, and freeze; add, when partly frozen, half a teacupful of whipped cream sweetened with a very slight dust of castor sugar. Freeze dry and mould in a Neapolitan box in the cave for about 1½ hours; then cut out in cutlet shapes. Dish on a border of iced cream, and iced cream for the centre; for this use 1 pint of cream, 1 dessert-spoonful of castor sugar, ditto of orange flower water, and a few drops of vanilla. Freeze dry and mould in a border mould.

10 ounces fresh spinach
Omit the soda.
1¼ cups milk
Cool the milk slightly.
3 or 4 egg yolks
2 tsp sugar
A pinch of salt
⅓ cup whipped cream sweetened
    with ½ tsp sugar
Neapolitan box:
    Substitute a loaf pan.
Cutlet shapes: oval
Border: a flat ring mold
FOR THE BORDER:
2½ cups cream
2 tsp sugar
2 tsp orange-flower water
¼ tsp vanilla

117.—Soufflés of Curry à la Ripon (*Petits Soufflés de Kari à la Ripon*).

Fry in about 2 ounces of fresh butter, 2 onions sliced, 2 sour apples, sprig of thyme, 2 bay leaves, sprig of parsley, about 1 ounce of cocoanut and 6 almonds blanched; to this add a raw or cooked sole or whiting. Fry all until a good golden colour, then add half a teaspoonful of curry powder, half a teaspoonful of curry paste, half a teaspoonful of tamarinds, little salt, and juice of 1 lemon; cover then with milk and cook till tender, add a little saffron yellow to

¼ cup butter
2 onions, sliced
2 tart apples, sliced
¼ tsp dried thyme
2 bay leaves
A sprig of parsley
¼ cup grated fresh coconut
6 almonds, blanched
1 sole or flounder
½ tsp curry powder
½ tsp curry paste:
    See Glossary.
½ tsp tamarind
Salt
The juice of 1 lemon
Milk to cover

Pound: Purée in blender or
     food processor.
¼ pint = ½ cup plus 2 Tb purée
½ cup plus 2 Tb whipped cream
Prawns: Large shrimp

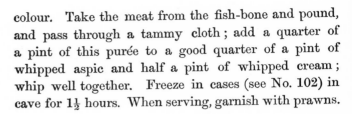

colour. Take the meat from the fish-bone and pound, and pass through a tammy cloth; add a quarter of a pint of this purée to a good quarter of a pint of whipped aspic and half a pint of whipped cream; whip well together. Freeze in cases (see No. 102) in cave for 1½ hours. When serving, garnish with prawns.

Aspic Jelly for No. 117.

Dissolve 2 ounces of Marshall's finest leaf gelatine (p. 64) in a quart of boiling water over the fire with 20 peppercorns, the juice of a lemon, a dessert-spoonful of salt, a small teacupful of vinegar, 1 onion, a little fresh tarragon (or a tablespoonful of tarragon vinegar), and a couple of bay leaves. Clear with the whites and shells of 2 eggs; strain off when it boils.

¼ cup powdered gelatin soaked 5
     minutes in 1 cup cold water
4 cups boiling water
20 peppercorns
The juice of 1 lemon
2 tsp salt
½ cup vinegar
1 onion
½ tsp dried tarragon
2 bay leaves
Whites and shells of 2 eggs
To clear: See Glossary.

THE ADVERTISEMENTS

in *The Book of Ices*, shown reduced on the following pages, are a treasure trove for the culinary historian. Here is information on the cost of equipment: a crank freezer, "ice cave", and mold to make a quart of ice cream cost over £3, the price of a made-to-measure dress. Here are the shapes of the molds Mrs. Marshall used; some of them survive unchanged to the present day, because the kitchen is a very conservative place. Here is help in reconstructing old recipes, too. For example, modern leaf gelatin comes in more than one strength; since Mrs. Marshall tells us, in her advertisement, that an ounce of her brand makes a quart (five cups U.S.) of aspic, we then know how much modern powdered gelatin to use. As Hyatt Mayor has written in the Foreword to this book, the trade catalogue is a unique record. As a cook I long to place an order. To begin with I'll take a dozen asparagus spears, three cucumbers, and a Number Two fluted-top ice pudding mold.

FOR PUDDINGS, BLANC-MANGE, CUSTARDS,

CHILDREN'S AND INVALIDS' DIET,

AND ALL THE USES OF ARROWROOT,

Brown & Polson's Corn Flour

HAS A WORLD-WIDE REPUTATION,

AND IS DISTINGUISHED FOR

UNIFORMLY SUPERIOR QUALITY.

NOTE.—Purchasers should insist on being supplied with **BROWN & POLSON'S CORN FLOUR.** Inferior qualities, asserting fictitious claims, are being offered for the sake of extra profit.

See Receipt No. 4, page 7 of this book.

MOULDS FOR ICE PUDDINGS.

All Ice Moulds are made in reputed measure.
PILLAR MOULDS.

No. 1.—FRUIT TOP.   No. 2.—FLUTED TOP.

½	1	1½	2	3 pints.
8s.	9s. 6d.	10s. 6d.	12s. 6d.	16s. each.

½	1	1½	2 pints.
8s. 6d.	9s. 6d.	10s. 6d.	12s. 6d. each.

No. 3.—ROSE TOP.   No. 4.—STEP TOP.

1	1½	2 pints.
9s. 6d.	10s. 6d.	12s. 6d. each.

½	1	1½	2 pints.
7s. 6d.	8s. 9d.	10s. 3d.	11s. 6d.

3 pints, 15s. 3d. each.

No. 5.—FLUTED TOP.

$\frac{1}{2}$ 1 $1\frac{1}{2}$ 2 pints.
7s. 6d.   8s. 9d.   10s. 3d.   11s. 6d. each.

No. 6.—CHERRY TOP.

1    $1\frac{1}{2}$ 2 pints.
9s. 6d.   10s. 6d.   12s. 6d. each.

No. 7.—WITH PLINTH.

2 pints, 13s. 6d. each.
3   ,,   16s.   ,,

No. 8.—WITH PLINTH.

2 pints, 13s. 6d. each.
3   ,,   16s.   ,,

No. 9.—VERY ORNA-MENTAL PLINTH.

2 pints, 13s. 6d. each.
3   ,,   16s.   ,,

No. 10.—ROSE TOP.

2 pints, 13s. 6d. each.
3   ,,   16s.   ,,

FANCY SHAPES.

No. 11.—REGISTERED.

1 pint, 10s. 6d. each.
2 pints, 14s.   ,,

No. 12.—GRAPE.
(Very bold and handsome.)

2 pints, 16s. each.
3   ,,   18s.   ,,
4   ,,   20s.   ,,

No. 13.—ASPARAGUS.

Height 5 inches, 1½ pints,
15s. 6d. each.

No. 14.—PLAIN MELON.

1½ pints, 16s. each.

No. 15.—SMALL BASKET.

1½ pints, 21s. each.

No. 16.—CHERRY TOP.

1 quart, 22s. 6d. each.

No. 17.—OVAL MELON.

7 inches long, 18s. 9d. each.

No. 18.—FRUIT BASKET.

1½ pints, 20s. each.

No. 19.—BASKET OF FRUITS.

Very handsome. 3 pints, 26s. each.

No. 20.—WHEATSHEAF.

8 inches high, 1 quart, 20s. each.

E

No. 21.—STAR. TOP.

No. 22.—SMALL PILLAR MOULD.

No. 23.—SMALL PILLAR.

3s. 9d. each.

4s. each.

4s. each.

No. 24.

No. 25.

No. 1	...	...	2s. 9d. each.	No. 1	...	...	2s. 9d. each.
„ 2	...	...	3s. 6d. „	„ 2	...	...	3s. 6d. „
„ 3	...	...	4s. 6d. „	„ 3	...	...	4s. 6d. „

No. 26.—FLUTED TOP.

No. 27.

No. 2	...	...	3s. 6d. each.	No. 2	...	...	3s. 6d. each.
„ 3	...	...	4s. 6d. „				

No. 28.—STEP TOP.

No. 29.—FISH.

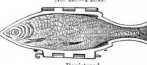

No. 1	...	...	2s. 9d. each.
„ 3	...	...	4s. 6d. „

Registered.
9s. 6d. each

No. 30.—CUCUMBER.

12½ inches long, 13s. 6d. each.

No. 31.—ASPARAGUS.

8¼ inches long, 3s. each.

No. 32.—GARNISHING OR DESSERT ICE MOULDS.

Grapes, Lemon, Artichoke, Gherkin, Strawberry, Peach, Plum, Pear,
Currant, Corn, Orange, Apricot, Fish, Oyster, Duck, Apple,
and many others.

1s. 9d. each.

NEAPOLITAN ICE MOULDS.

No. 33.—TIN.

7 in. by 3½ in. by 1¾ in. 2s. 6d. each.

No. 34.—ROSE TOP (PEWTER)

8½ in. by 3½ in. by 5⅛ in. 16s. each.

No. 35.—PEWTER.

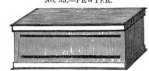

No. 1 ... ... 8s. 6d. each.   No. 2 ... ... 12s. each.

TIN ICE MOULDS.

No. 36.—ICE PUDDING, SHOWING SHAPE PRODUCED.

No. 1	...	...	1 pint, 4s. 8d.	No. 4	...	...	3 pints, 6s. 8d.
No. 2	...	...	1½ „ 5s. 0d.	„ 5	...	...	4 „ 8s. 9d.
No. 3	...	...	2 „ 5s. 4d.				

No. 37.

No. 38.

No. 1	...	...	1 pint, 4s. 0d.	No. 1	...	...	1 pint, 2s. 8d.
„ 2	...	...	1½ „ 4s. 4d.	„ 2	...	...	1½ „ 2s. 11d.
„ 3	...	...	2 „ 4s. 8d.	„ 3	...	...	2 „ 3s. 2d.
„ 4	...	...	3 „ 6s. 0d.	„ 4	...	...	3 „ 3s. 6d.
„ 5	...	...	4 „ 6s. 8d.				

No. 39.

| No. 1 | ... | ... | 1½ pints, 4s. 4d. | No. 2 | ... | ... | 3 pints, 5s. 4d. |
| | | | No. 3 | ... | .... | 4 pints, 6s. 4d. |

No. 40.　54　No. 41.

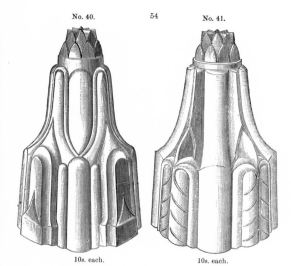

10s. each.　　　10s. each.

COVER AND PIPE FOR ABOVE MOULDS.

55

ICE POTS

(PEWTER AND ZINC),

AND

SUPERIOR OAK TUBS

WITH GALVANIZED HOOPS.

MADE OF WELL-SEASONED OAK AND VERY STRONG.

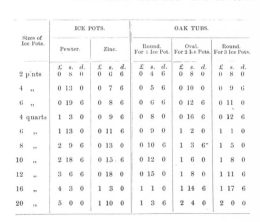

Sizes of Ice Pots.	ICE POTS.		OAK TUBS.		
	Pewter.	Zinc.	Round. For 1 Ice Pot.	Oval. For 2 Ice Pots.	Round. For 3 Ice Pots.
	£ s. d.	£ s. d.	£ s. d.	£ s. d.	£ s. d.
2 p'nts	0 8 0	0 6 6	0 4 6	0 8 0	0 8 0
4 ,,	0 13 0	0 7 6	0 5 6	0 10 0	0 9 6
6 ,,	0 19 6	0 8 6	0 6 6	0 12 6	0 11 0
4 quarts	1 3 0	0 9 6	0 8 0	0 16 6	0 12 6
6 ,,	1 13 0	0 11 6	0 9 0	1 2 0	1 1 0
8 ,,	2 9 6	0 13 0	0 10 6	1 3 6	1 5 0
10 ,,	2 18 6	0 15 6	0 12 0	1 6 0	1 8 0
12 ,,	3 6 6	0 18 0	0 15 0	1 8 0	1 11 6
16 ,,	4 3 0	1 3 0	1 1 0	1 14 6	1 17 6
20 ,,	5 0 0	1 10 0	1 3 6	2 4 0	2 0 0

MARSHALL'S PATENT FREEZER.

Complete View.

IS PRAISED BY ALL WHO KNOW IT FOR

CHEAPNESS in first cost. CLEANLINESS in working.
ECONOMY in use. SIMPLICITY in construction.
RAPIDITY in Freezing.

NO PACKING NECESSARY. NO SPATULA NECESSARY.

Smooth and delicious Ice produced in 3 minutes.

SIZES—No. 1, to freeze any quantity up to one qt., £1 5 0.
No. 2, for two qts., £1 15 0. No. 3, for four qts., £3 0 0. No. 4,
for six qts., £4 0 0. Larger sizes to order.

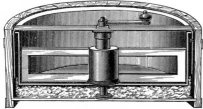

Vertical Section.

Showing the fan inside, which remains still while the pan revolves
and scrapes up the film of ice as it forms on the bottom of the pan.
The ice and salt is also shown *under* the pan; there is no need to
pack any round the sides.

Can be ordered direct from MARSHALL'S SCHOOL OF COOKERY,
or through any Ironmonger.

MARSHALL'S PATENT ICE CAVE.

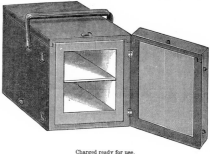

Charged ready for use.

USES.

FOR SETTING ICE PUDDINGS without the use of grease or
chance of brine entering, and without the expense of special moulds.
Ice puddings when moulded can be turned out and kept ready for use
at any minute, so that the ice can be made and held ready before com-
mencing to serve the dinner if necessary.

FOR FREEZING SOUFFLÉS it offers great advantages, as the
progress of freezing can be examined from time to time. The soufflés
can always be kept ready for use.

FOR INVALIDS to have always at hand a supply of ice or iced
food or drink, or for food or drink to be kept hot for any length of time.
It is especially useful in nurseries, in the latter respect.

FOR CONFECTIONERS to send out ice puddings, etc., quite
ready for serving; for keeping ice creams, etc., ready for selling.

FOR KEEPING ICES during Balls, Evening and Garden
Parties, and for taking ice creams, etc., to Races, Picnics, etc.

AND FOR REFRIGERATORS GENERALLY.

SIZE No. 1 will hold one quart mould. Size 2, two quart moulds.
Size 3, four quart moulds. Size 4 will hold six large champagne
bottles. Sizes No. 2 and upwards can be used for icing mineral waters,
etc., and kept in dining, smoking, and billiard rooms.

PRICES.

No. 1, £1 11s. 6d. No. 2, £2 2s. No. 3, £3 3s. No. 4,
£4 4s. Larger and special sizes to order.

BY ROYAL LETTERS PATENT.
MARSHALL'S PATENT ICE CAVE.

Lid off ready for charging.

When the front door is closed the apparatus has the appearance of a cabinet which can be lifted by a handle fixed to the sides and passing over the top. When the door is open, nothing is seen except the internal cave and its contents (see page 57).

If the interstices between the cave and the metal casing be properly filled with a mixture of two parts ice and one of salt, so great is the cold produced in the internal cave that it will freeze a quantity of water placed in the inner cave into a solid mass, and the temperature produced will stand for some hours at 32 degrees of frost. If instead of ice and salt only ice be used, the temperature in the cupboard will remain at freezing point.

Though Ice Cave has been the name given to this invention, it can also be used for keeping food, etc., hot. By filling the space between the metals with boiling water, a high degree of temperature is maintained in the cupboard. The machine was charged with boiling water at 4 p.m., and a vessel containing water at 140 degrees was placed in the cupboard. At 10 p.m. this water stood at 115 degrees, and at 8 a.m. on the following morning, or after sixteen hours in a cold room in November, it stood at 80 degrees.

Both on the body of the machine and on the door there is a screw plug fixed, by means of which the brine, water, etc., can be drawn off from between the metals, thus rendering it possible to recharge the machine without disturbing the contents of the cupboard. It will be perceived, therefore, that by recharging the machine when necessary a high or low degree of temperature can be maintained for any length of time whatever.

IMPROVED ICE BREAKER.

No. 1.

For Hotel Keepers, Confectioners, Wine Merchants, Refreshment Rooms, Ships' Cabins, Butlers' Pantries, etc., etc.

Size A.—Price £5 ; with Drawer, £5 10s.

„ B.—Price £6 ; „ „ £6 10s.

IMPROVED ICE BREAKER.

No. 2, OPEN FRAME.

For Fish Merchants, Fishmongers, Fishing Smacks, Refreshment Contractors, Ice Cream Makers, etc., etc.

Sizes	A	B	C	D	E
Prices	£9 9s.	£10 10s.	£11 11s.	£13 13s.	£14 14s.
Crushing power per hour	2	3	4	6	8 tons.

IMPROVED ICE BREAKER.

No. 3, BOX FRAME.

This has a store underneath, about 4ft. 6in. by 2ft. 3in., and a drawer in front.

Sizes	A	B	C	D	E
Prices	£10 10s.	£11 11s.	£12 12s.	£14 14s.	£15 15s.
Crushing power per hour	2	3	4	6	8 tons.

PURE FRUIT AND LIQUEUR SYRUPS.

In Bottles, 1s. each.

For making Ice Creams, Water Ices, Summer Drinks, Jellies, etc.

FRUITS.		LIQUEURS.
Cherry,	*Pine-apple,*	*Noyeau,*
Raspberry,	*Pear,*	*Curaçoa,*
Strawberry,	*Lemon,*	*Kirsch,*
Red Currant,	*Orange.*	*Maraschino.*

These Liqueur Syrups are identical in flavour with the Foreign Liqueurs, but, being without the spirit, are superior for culinary purposes, and cost about one-tenth as much.

See that every bottle bears the name and full address,

A. B. MARSHALL, 30, Mortimer Street.

PRESERVED WHOLE FRUITS FOR ICES.

Finest Brands only.

IN BOTTLES.

				s.	d.	
Raspberries ...	...	...	...	1	6	per bott.
Strawberries	...	...	...	1	6	,,
Greengages ...	...	...	...	1	6	,,
Cherries ...	...	...	...	1	6	,,
Ditto, without stones		...	...	2	0	,,
Pears, white or red		...	...	1	6	,,
Currants, ditto	...	...	...	1	6	,,
Apricots ...	...	...	...	2	0	,,
Sliced Pine ...	...	...	...	2	0	,,
Peaches, peeled ...	...	...	...	2	6	,,

IN TINS.

Apricots	...	...	...	...	1	9	per tin.
Peaches ...	...	...	...	1	9	,,
Pine-apple	...	...	...	...	1	9	,,

MARSHALL'S FREEZING SALT.

Produces more intense cold than any other. Bags, 6d. each.

PURE HARMLESS VEGETABLE COLOURS

FOR

COLOURING ICES, CREAMS, JELLIES, ETC.

PASTE COLOURS, 1s. per Bottle.

CHERRY RED, APPLE GREEN, COFFEE BROWN, APRICOT YELLOW, DAMSON BLUE.

LIQUID COLOURS, 8d. per Bottle.

SAFFRON, CARMINE, SAP GREEN.

If transparency is required (as in jellies), use the liquid colours; in other cases, either liquid or paste may be used.

Every bottle is stamped with name—

A. B. MARSHALL.

CONCENTRATED ESSENCES,

8d. PER BOTTLE.

VANILLA, ALMONDS, LEMON, RATAFIA, PEAR, PINE-APPLE, BANANA, CITRON.

The above Syrups, Colours, and Essences can be ordered direct or through any Grocer.

ORANGE FLOWER WATER,

6d. and 1s. PER BOTTLE.

SACCHAROMETER,

For testing the strength of the Syrup.

3s. 6d. each, in box.

Tammy Cloth. Very best ...	...	2s. 3d. per yard.
,, Spoons ...	...	9d. and 1s. each.
White Horsehair Sieves	1s. 8d., 2s. 2d., 3s. 3d., and 4s. each.
Soufflé Cases ...	...	5d. and 6d. per doz.
Whisks, with wood handle ...	...	9d. each.
,, with wire-thread handles	...	1s. 3d. and 1s. 6d. each.
Ice Spoons. German Silver.	...	2s. per doz.
,, Nickel Silver ...	3s. 6d., 4s. 6d., and 6s. per doz.
,, Plated on Nickel A 1	13s., 16s., 24s., and 28s. per doz.
Glass Ice Dishes ...	6s., 9s., 12s., 16s., 20s., and 24s. per doz.
Soufflé Dishes. Plated on Best Nickel	...	70s. each.

MARSHALL'S
FINEST LEAF GELATINE.
USED BY ALL THE BEST CHEFS.

Can be ordered through any Grocer. Quantities of 2 lbs. and over forwarded to any address in the United Kingdom. Post free on receipt of Postal Order.

In Cardboard Boxes only, with name and address,
1 lb. 2s. 6d., ½ lb. 1s. 4d., ¼ lb. 9d., 1 oz. 3d.

One ounce packet makes a quart of magnificent jelly equal to that made from Calves' feet. Recipe for use with each packet.

It dissolves immediately in hot water and needs no soaking.

Beware of Coarse and Impure Imitations.

MARSHALL'S
SUPERFINE FELT JELLY BAGS.

		Size No. 10.	No. 12.	No. 15.
Without Seam.	Various sizes.	3s.	3s. 8d.	4s. 4d.

Post Free 3d. extra for each.

EVERY BAG IS STAMPED WITH NAME AND SIZE.

Any of the above may be ordered direct or through any Grocer.

A. B. MARSHALL,
30, Mortimer Street, London, W.

GLOSSARY

Almonds, sweet and bitter: Sweet almonds are the variety generally available in markets in this country. The intensely flavored bitter almond, still used in Europe, may be replaced by a discreet quantity of almond extract (⅛ to ¼ teaspoon). Imitation bitter-almond flavoring, imported from Germany, can be found in specialty food shops.

Almond essence: Almond extract.

Angelica is a biennial plant whose hollow green stalks are candied, sliced, and cut into ornamental shapes to decorate food. It is also used to flavor liqueurs.

Banana essence is still available.

Bergamot essence: Mrs. Marshall probably means essence of the bergamot orange, since she uses it in an orange water ice. There is also a bergamot pear, and the herb bergamot (*Monarda didyma*), which is better known as Oswego tea.

Biscuit: Any plain, unsweetened biscuit can be used, or the cook may wish to try the following recipe from Mrs. Beeton, *The Book of Household Management* (1861): "Crisp Biscuits. Ingredients.—1 lb. of flour, the yolk of 1 egg, milk. *Mode.*—Mix the flour and the yolk of the egg with sufficient milk to make the whole into a very stiff paste; beat it well, and knead it until it is perfectly smooth. Roll the paste out *very thin;* with a round cutter shape it into small biscuits, and bake them a nice brown in a slow oven from 12 to 18 minutes. Time.— 12 to 18 minutes. *Average cost,* 4d. *Seasonable* at any time."

"Break, or crack, the stones": This was a common technique used to extract the flavor from fruit pits. Mrs. Marshall uses it with peaches, apricots, cherries, and plums. You may substitute ⅛ to ¼ teaspoon of almond extract, or ½ tablespoon of crème de noyeau, or a suitable fruit brandy.

Cedrat: The citrus fruit of the citron tree, shaped like a lemon but as large as a grapefruit. Only the rind is used, and it is always candied. In the United States it is usually sold diced or in chunks. In recipes 18 and 68 the cook may substitute ¼ cup finely chopped citron for the sugar lumps rubbed on the citron skins, or any other proportion suitable to the needs of a particular occasion.

Cherry, Kentish: This is the red morello, a juicy sour cooking cherry.

"Clear with the whites and shells of two eggs": Crush the shells, beat the whites until foamy, and add both whites and shells to the cooled liquid mixture. Then heat slowly until it has just begun to simmer. Hold it at this temperature for five minutes, and then strain it through a dampened cheesecloth. If the aspic is not entirely clear, the process may be repeated. However, since in recipes 115 and 117 it is subsequently mixed with other ingredients, crystal clarity is unnecessary.

Coconut: If coconuts are not available, you may make a mildly-coconut-flavored custard by warming 2½ cups of unsweetened coconut in 2½ cups each of milk and light cream gently for half an hour. Keep covered; do not let the mixture simmer or boil. You may wish to reinforce the coconut effect by adding a tablespoon of the grated coconut to the ice-cream mixture before freezing. Do not substitute sweetened coconut. It contains far too much sugar, which can prevent your ice cream from freezing. The three brands of imitation coconut flavoring I have tried do not approach the flavor of real coconut at all.

Colorings: Mrs. Marshall uses color to excess, by twentieth-century standards. In some cases food colorings may be needed, but usually two or three drops will suffice. As air is churned into a mixture during the freezing process, its color will become lighter. The cautious cook will err on the side of delicacy.

Corn flour is a special preparation of wheat starch. An equal quantity of cornstarch may be substituted.

Crack the stones: See break the stones.

Cream: Use light or medium cream unless an especially rich ice cream is desired. Whipped cream is measured after whipping; ¾ cup of unwhipped cream will usually yield about 1¼ cups of whipped cream.

Curry paste: When I tested Soufflés of Curry à la Ripon, I omitted the curry paste and increased the curry powder porportionately. To satisfy the reader's curiosity, however, here is a recipe from a contemporary source. Coriander, tumeric, and cumin seeds are widely sold already ground; it should be remembered that English "corn" is American "wheat." Both sweet oil and mustard oil may be found in stores specializing in Indian foods.

From T. F. Garrett's *Encyclopaedia of Practical Cookery* (189–): "Put into a mortar ½ lb. of roasted coriander-seeds, 1 oz. of roasted cumin-seeds, 2 oz. each of black pepper, dry chillies, dry tumeric, and mustard-seeds, 1 oz. each of dry ginger and garlic, and 4 oz. each of sugar, salt, and roasted corn (gram däl), and pound well, pour in sufficient white-wine vinegar to bring the mixture to the consistence of jelly. Warm some sweet-oil in a pan, and as soon as it commences to bubble, drop in the mixture and fry until it is reduced to a paste. When this is cold, put it in bottles, cork them, and keep in a dry place until wanted for use. Mustard-oil may be substituted for the sweet-oil, but on no account must any water be allowed to get into the paste, or it will be spoilt."

Damsons: Small tart purple cooking plums.

Filberts: Domestic hazelnuts. In Mrs. Marshall's day the best came from Spain and were therefore called Spanish nuts.

Ginger: Mrs. Marshall uses several forms, all of which are still available. Preserved ginger comes in two forms: in a syrup and crystallized. In testing these recipes I have used the latter. Ginger brandy and a variety of ginger wine, made with green ginger and currants, are both available today.

Gelatine, leaf gelatine: Powdered gelatin may be substituted at the rate of 1 level tablespoon or 1 envelope per (U.S.) pint of liquid.

Lemon essence: Lemon extract.

Liqueurs: Kirsch, maraschino and crème de noyeau are all manufactured today. Do not attempt to substitute maraschino syrup for the real, colorless liqueur. Noyeau, made from peach kernels, has a character all its own; if unobtainable, ⅛ teaspoon of almond extract or a few drops of imitation bitter-almond flavoring may be substituted.

Mixed spice: From T. F. Garrett's *Encyclopaedia of Practical Cookery* (189–): "Pound 2 oz. each of allspice, cloves, and cinnamon, ½ oz. each of nutmeg and ginger, and 2 oz. of coriander-seeds. When they are well powdered they must be kept in a well-stoppered bottle."

Paper soufflé cases: See Introduction, p. xxv.

Ratafia biscuits: When I tested Mrs. Marshall's recipe for ratafia cream ice, I first used good-quality modern macaroons from a bakery. It was the only occasion on which I had a total failure; the ice cream was too sweet to freeze solid. Then I made it with Mrs. Beeton's ratafia biscuits, halving the recipe, and it turned out very nicely. I used sweet almonds, almond extract, a few drops of imitation bitter-almond flavoring, ¾ cup of sugar, and 2 egg whites. In place of a biscuit syringe, the cook may use a pastry bag and tube with a nozzle measuring about ¼ inch, or the batter may simply be dropped from a teaspoon. For cartridge paper substitute parchment paper.

From Mrs. Beeton, *The Book of Household Management* (1861): "Ingredients.— ½ lb. of sweet almonds, ¼ lb. of bitter ones, ¾ lb. of sifted loaf sugar, the whites of 4 eggs. *Mode.*—Blanch, skin, and dry the almonds, and pound them in a mortar with the white of an egg; stir in the sugar, and